T0295950

Philosophy and Leadership

Today, managers, politicians, educators, and healthcare providers are highly skilled technicians who navigate modern systems. However, followers seek more than know-how; they desire moral leadership. Even leaders equipped with skills must make difficult ethical choices.

This book connects philosophy to leadership by examining three representative texts from the history of philosophy: Plato's *Republic*, Aristotle's *Nicomachean Ethics*, and Niccolò Machiavelli's *The Prince*. The leadership ideas contained in each one of these philosopher's works not only were pioneering for their age but also continue to be relevant today because they provide insight into the enduring questions of leadership. The book demonstrates the timeliness of the classical works by applying these philosophical approaches to historical and contemporary cases.

This book is ideal for readers who are acquainted with philosophy and those who are uninitiated. The connections made between philosophy, leadership literature, and real-life leaders enable readers to appreciate how deeper reflection into the themes of leadership might merit scholarly attention and bear witness to the close union between the philosophy of leadership and the real world.

Brent Edwin Cusher is Associate Professor in the Department of Leadership and American Studies at Christopher Newport University, USA.

Mark Antonio Menaldo is Department Head and Associate Professor of Liberal Studies at Texas A&M University-Commerce, USA.

Leadership Horizons
Series Editors:
John R. Shoup
California Baptist University, USA
Troy Hinrichs
California Baptist University, USA

The original and timeless research on leadership is situated in the classical works associated with the humanities. Great literature, art, theatre, philosophy, and music provide both existential and visceral insights to the drama of leadership beyond what traditional approaches to leadership studies have been able to furnish up to now. The classics in the humanities are didactic commentaries on universal themes associated with the challenges and hopes of good leadership. Knowledge of the classics provides a way of appreciating historical and contemporary cultures and a framework for thinking deeply about what is true, good, honorable, and beautiful. Returning the classics to the leadership genre equips leaders with a culturally informed language and narrative to develop the often ignored aesthetical aspects of leadership. This series connects lessons from various great works in art, literature, philosophy, theatre, and music to specific leadership research and contemporary leadership challenges. The series weaves the art and science of leadership studies and equips readers with multiple frames of reference to become aesthetically pleasing, engaging, and culturally astute leaders to make the right things happen the right way.

Leadership Horizons is relevant to students and researchers across business and management, organizational and institutional studies, and the humanities.

Books in the series

Literature and Leadership
The Role of Narrative in Organizational Sensemaking
John R. Shoup and Troy Hinrichs

Philosophy and Leadership
Three Classical Models and Cases
Brent Edwin Cusher and Mark Antonio Menaldo

Philosophy and Leadership
Three Classical Models and Cases

**Brent Edwin Cusher
and Mark Antonio Menaldo**

Routledge
Taylor & Francis Group

LONDON AND NEW YORK

First published 2021
by Routledge
2 Park Square, Milton Park, Abingdon, Oxon OX14 4RN

and by Routledge
605 Third Avenue, New York, NY 10158

Routledge is an imprint of the Taylor & Francis Group, an informa business

British Library Cataloguing-in-Publication Data
A catalogue record for this book is available from the British Library

Library of Congress Cataloging-in-Publication Data
Names: Cusher, Brent Edwin, 1978– author. | Menaldo, Mark Antonio,
    1979– author.
Title: Philosophy and leadership : three classical models and cases / Brent
    Edwin Cusher and Mark Antonio Menaldo.
Description: 1 Edition. | New York : Routledge, 2021. | Series: Leadership
    horizons | Includes bibliographical references and index.
Identifiers: LCCN 2021005577 (print) | LCCN 2021005578 (ebook) |
    ISBN 9780367425586 (hardback) | ISBN 9781032046099 (paperback) |
    ISBN 9780367853433 (ebook)
Subjects: LCSH: Leadership. | Leadership—Philosophy.
Classification: LCC HD57.7 .C874 2021 (print) | LCC HD57.7 (ebook) |
    DDC 658.4001—dc23
LC record available at https://lccn.loc.gov/2021005577
LC ebook record available at https://lccn.loc.gov/2021005578

ISBN: 978-0-367-42558-6 (hbk)
ISBN: 978-1-032-04609-9 (pbk)
ISBN: 978-0-367-85343-3 (ebk)

Typeset in Times New Roman
by Apex CoVantage, LLC

We dedicate this book to George and Carolyn Cusher, and Victor and Frances Menaldo, our parents.

Contents

Acknowledgments

We must give thanks to the editors of the *Leadership Horizons* series, John R. Shoup and Troy W. Hinrichs, for their enthusiastic support during all the phases of writing this book. Many thanks to the editors from Routledge – Rebecca Marsh, Sophie Peoples, Naomi Round Cahalin, and Brianna Ascher – who have made the experience an easy and pleasant one for its writers. We are grateful to the College of Social Sciences Research Workshop participants at Christopher Newport University, as well as to Andrew Baker and Lucas Allen. They all provided invaluable suggestions for improvement on our Aristotle chapter. For financial assistance, we also thank the Institute for Humane Studies at George Mason University for their generous support through the Hayek Fund for Scholars, and the Office of the President at Texas A&M University-Commerce. Last, we would like to thank Emma Harris for her invaluable assistance in the final preparation of the manuscript and index.

1 The love of wisdom and the philosopher's quest to understand humanity

In this book, we make an earnest attempt to apply the discipline of philosophy, and certain important texts in the history of philosophy, to the systematic study of leadership. Our hope is that its publication can achieve a number of practical aims. The book is designed, for instance, to be useful for both teachers and practitioners of leadership who may not necessarily have much experience with philosophic texts and ideas, yet who are eager to integrate such resources into their teaching or leadership practice. The history of western philosophy is most definitely large and complex, and certain works in this tradition can be difficult to understand – some of them notoriously so. Yet that should not be an impediment to having these works bear on matters of leadership in the contemporary world. We aim to show how philosophic works can be generally applicable to leadership in many contexts, including business, politics, society, culture, the globalized world, and others. Since philosophy is essential to the task of making sound moral judgments, our book stresses how attention to these texts and ideas can help both teachers and practitioners understand, and therefore negotiate, the difficult ethical issues of leadership – these "dynamics that make the heart of leadership tick," as Joanne Ciulla has so memorably said.[1]

Furthermore, despite the academic field of leadership studies having been largely dominated, since its inception, by the methods and research of the social sciences, works from humanities disciplines like philosophy can make a contribution to the conversation that is deep, rich, and capable of providing unique insight into the dynamics between leaders and followers.[2]

---

1 Joanne B. Ciulla, ed., *Ethics, the Heart of Leadership*, 2nd ed. (Westport, CT: Praeger, 2004), xix.
2 For similar thoughts, consider Jean Bethke Elshtain, "Leadership and the Humanities," in *Leadership and the Liberal Arts: Achieving the Promise of a Liberal Education*, ed. J. Thomas Wren, Ronald E. Riggio, and Michael A. Genovese (New York: Palgrave Macmillan, 2009), 117–25; and Antonio Marturano, J. Thomas Wren, and Michael Harvey,

While the field is not utterly lacking in voices from the humanities, still they have had a relatively small role to play in the broad body of literature. Similar to the other authors in the *Leadership Horizons* series, we hope that our book will serve as a persuasive example, perhaps even a model, of what such humanities-based contributions could look like.

That said, and to underscore what we have just implied, the large body of literature on leadership and followership is not entirely devoid of works from a philosophic perspective, or that discuss philosophers and their ideas in some way. Many of these sources center on theories of ethical decision making, while others explore directly what certain philosophers can explain to us about leadership.[3] Why, then, another book in this particular vein? What do we intend to offer in this book that is fresh, so that it can claim to have a suitable place within the wider literature? In our book, we have chosen to highlight three representative texts from the history of philosophy, an examination of which will make up the lion's share of our presentation. These works are Plato's *Republic*, Aristotle's *Nicomachean Ethics*, and Niccolò Machiavelli's *The Prince*. Unlike most other works on philosophy and leadership, ours self-consciously provides an in-depth and careful reading of each of these texts, sticking to the writings themselves as closely as possible so as to establish a firm ground for our interpretation. We believe that there are certain books that can rightfully be considered "great," not so much because they were written by such-and-such a person, but because they contain profound discussions of the most important problems that humans confront in leadership. The *Republic*, the *Nicomachean Ethics*, and *The Prince* are three such books, as we intend to show. We are particularly interested in clarifying how the philosophers themselves would

---

"Editorial: The Making of *Leadership and the Humanities*," *Leadership and the Humanities* 1, no. 1 (2013): 1–5.

3 Works on leadership and ethical philosophy include: Jessica Flanigan, "Philosophical Methodology and Leadership Ethics," *Leadership* 14, no. 6 (2018): 707–30; Nannerl O. Keohane, *Thinking about Leadership* (Princeton, NJ: Princeton University Press, 2012), 194–223; Terry L. Price, *Leadership and the Ethics of Influence* (New York: Routledge, 2020); Terry L. Price, *Understanding Ethical Failures in Leadership* (New York: Cambridge University Press, 2006); and Alejo José G. Sison, *The Moral Capital of Leaders: Why Virtue Matters* (Northampton, UK: Edward Elgar, 2004). Works that focus on what certain philosophers can explain to us about leadership include: Brent Edwin Cusher and Mark A. Menaldo, eds., *Leadership and the Unmasking of Authenticity: The Philosophy of Self-Knowledge and Deception* (Northampton, UK: Edward Elgar, 2018); Rita Gardiner, "Gender, Authenticity, and Leadership: Thinking with Arendt," *Leadership* 12, no. 5 (2016): 632–7; Nathan W. Harter, *Foucault on Leadership* (New York: Routledge, 2016); and John Lawler and Ian Ashman, "Theorizing Leadership Authenticity: A Sartrean Perspective," *Leadership* 8, no. 4 (2012): 327–44.

have wanted to be understood, articulating that perspective on leaders and followers to a contemporary audience concerned with these issues.

In most cases, moreover, it is absolutely necessary to stick closely to the texts themselves in order to fully understand what the philosopher has meant to say. Doubtless, this procedure can seem daunting. In some quarters, works of philosophy have developed the reputation of being impossible to penetrate, or being long, grueling, and fundamentally boring slogs to get through, with the end result being only more confusion in the mind of the reader. How many potential readers have been turned away, however unfortunately, from philosophy by the sight of weighty tomes like Aristotle's *Metaphysics*, Georg Hegel's *Phenomenology of Spirit*, or Martin Heidegger's *Being and Time*? The truth, though, is that the vast majority of writers in the march of western philosophy were not only profound thinkers but also artful, even beautiful, writers, certainly on par with some of the best authors of literature we have. Some of these authors – and Plato, Aristotle, and Machiavelli (not to mention Hegel and Heidegger!) fit this characterization perfectly – did not set their deepest thoughts on the surface of their writings. Rather, they skillfully composed works that are intended to draw readers in with their charm, wit, and beauty. The philosophers hold out the promise of liberally repaying serious attention to their words, as well as to multiple readings of their words. Our approach, which pays careful and sustained attention to the three texts themselves, should pay significant dividends.

In order to make our interpretations of these writings more accessible to readers, not to mention more applicable to the concerns of leaders and followers, we have provided a number of relevant case studies in the following pages. The cases will benefit teachers, insofar as they contain analyses of pertinent examples that can be used when making the practical application of philosophy to leadership. Our hope is that readers will find them useful for another reason too, since it may be possible to see the details of what Plato, Aristotle, or Machiavelli is saying more lucidly by reference to contemporary cases of leadership – cases that are, of course, more widely known. Yet our intention with the material on specific cases is to come at it with an even wider scope. Not only have we included, in Chapter 5, an example that one can plausibly associate with the leadership ideas from each philosopher, we have also written brief case studies of individuals who are, in some manner, historically related to the philosophers themselves: Dion of Syracuse, Alexander the Great, and Cesare Borgia. In doing this, we hope that readers with a strong interest in history will find such sections both engaging and useful. Moreover, we hope that all readers will come to see the timeless quality of the leadership insights we are exploring.

Philosophy as a discipline and philosophy as love of wisdom

It is only natural that this discussion, so far, has begged a number of important questions. What precisely is meant by the term "philosophy"? Where does this thing called philosophy come from, and what does it aim at? In short, what are we really talking about when we attempt to associate works of the "philosophers" to the practical project of leadership, as well as to our understanding of leadership in all of its remarkable dynamics? The answers to these questions are not always straightforward, but it is essential to move ahead with as clear a definition of the terms as we can muster.

Earlier, we noted that philosophy is a humanities discipline, a simple truth that leads to an even more basic observation: philosophy has come to be one of the traditional academic disciplines, such that most colleges and universities in the United States are home to a designated department of philosophy. The composition of these units is made up mostly of scholars who have earned a doctoral degree in a similar university department. If a particular institution does not have a stand-alone department of philosophy, it likely still offers a major in the subject.[4] As is the case with most academic disciplines, philosophy houses a number of subfields supported by scholars working in those areas. According to the website of the American Philosophical Association, the "broadest subfields of philosophy are most commonly taken to be logic, ethics, metaphysics, epistemology, and the history of philosophy."[5] Logic is the study of argumentation and reason, whereas ethics concerns questions of morality and character. Students of metaphysics examine the structure of being, and epistemology investigates knowledge and the process whereby we come to know things. The history of philosophy, finally, considers what philosophers have said and done in the past, both for its own sake and for supporting the other fields of philosophical inquiry.[6]

Now, despite our singular focus so far on departments of philosophy, it is true that many of these same subjects are treated in other areas of academia.

---

4 For these thoughts and more, see Eric Schwitzgebel, "What Kinds of Universities Lack Philosophy Departments? Some Data," *Daily Nous*, March 22, 2017, http://dailynous.com/2017/03/22/kinds-universities-lack-philosophy-departments-data-guest-post-eric-schwitzgebel/.

5 Robert Audi, "The Field of Philosophy," *Philosophy: A Brief Guide for Undergraduates: The American Philosophical Association*, 2017, accessed January 6, 2021, www.apaonline.org/page/undergraduates.

6 There is a body of literature the size of an ocean for each one of these subfields, and it would be impossible to provide an adequate bibliography here. For those interested in learning more about these and other areas, Routledge Press has published a series of accessible books. Consider, e.g., Robert Audi, *Epistemology: A Contemporary Introduction to the Theory of Knowledge*, 3rd ed. (New York: Routledge, 2010); Harry J. Gensler, *Ethics: A Contemporary Introduction*, 3rd ed. (New York: Routledge, 2017); and Michael J. Loux and Thomas M. Crisp, *Metaphysics: A Contemporary Introduction*, 4th ed. (New York: Routledge, 2017).

For instance, one of the major subfields of the discipline of political science is political theory or political philosophy, in which scholars pursue a great many of the same questions, as well as study and teach many of the same texts, as one finds in departments of philosophy.[7] Yet this quick and seemingly idle observation leads to another – one that may sound strange but is not intended to be controversial in any real way. In an important sense, the overwhelming majority of scholars working at academic institutions, both in the United States and across the world, conduct their work in philosophy. This understanding of philosophy is perhaps more spacious, but it is not necessarily flawed   indeed, it is likely closer to the original meaning of philosophy, as we will go on to describe in our chapter on Plato's *Republic*. Here is one very simple example to illustrate the point: at almost all colleges and universities, in order to be a full member of the teaching and research faculty, one must have the terminal degree in her or his field. And for the most part, that means that professors have been awarded a Ph.D. by an institution, a degree title that stands for the Latin term *philosophiae doctor*, or doctor of philosophy. Despite the fact that most people think only of medical doctors when hearing the term "doctor," the word derives from the Latin *docere* (to teach) and means, most simply, one with the knowledge to teach a discipline. But that discipline is, in this case, philosophy: *philosophiae doctor*. In other words, regardless of whether such-and-such a Ph.D.-holding professor is in a department of English, or Biology, or Classical Languages, or Leadership and American Studies, or Psychology, the professor is and should be a "philosopher," meaning a lover of wisdom, a term that derives from two Greek words: *philia* (love) and *sophia* (wisdom). This person has become so, in part, by having been liberally educated in both undergraduate and graduate schooling, and this person devotes his or her life to activities that are consistent with the love of wisdom.

A brief, all-too-brief, history of philosophy

And so, there is a larger notion of philosophy – the love of wisdom – that applies to a scope much wider than what happens in the specific academic discipline of philosophy. In our book's project of applying philosophy to leadership, we strive to take this larger conception into account. Now, the story of the development of philosophy as the love of wisdom is both extensive and complex. If scholars devote whole careers to studying and researching the history of philosophy, one of the basic subfields of the discipline, then we surely get a sense for just how extensive and complex this

---

7 For a representative work, see Leo Strauss and Joseph Cropsey, eds., *History of Political Philosophy*, 3rd ed. (Chicago: University of Chicago Press, 1987).

history is. In what follows, however, we take a crack at providing a very basic sketch of it so that readers of this book can view the broad contours. Our hope is that readers will appreciate just how many colorful and diverse elements of the story will unfortunately be missed. That said, the brief discussion that follows can potentially assist them in making sense of where Plato, Aristotle, and Machiavelli – our chosen guides for leadership – fit into the trajectory of western philosophy.[8]

Philosophy was born and grew in the wider world of ancient Greece. The first philosopher recognized by historians is Thales, a man who lived in the seventh and sixth centuries BC in Miletus, a city in Asia Minor. Thales challenged the worldview that saw the cosmos, that is, the whole of nature, as a mysterious creation and government of the gods. He sought rather to use his own rational capacities to locate the essential principle of nature in one basic substance, and in his view, this substance was water. Thales was, however, not the only one investigating nature in such a way. Indeed, an important unifying feature of these early philosophers is that they pursued knowledge of the essential principles of the natural world. For instance, Heraclitus of Ephesus, another city in Asia Minor, taught that the world was unified by *logos*, meaning "word" or "reason," and that the essential element of the cosmos was fire. He famously said *panta rhei*, or "everything flows" – a description of nature that emphasizes its impermanence and changeability. Pythagoras and his followers living in the south of Italy held, by contrast, that number provides the basic structure for the universe. Scholars group many others of these early philosophers into a category called sophists, meaning men who investigated the principles of nature but who also taught students for a fee. Protagoras, one of the most well-known of the sophists, famously taught a kind of relativism with his statement "man is the measure of all things, of things that are as to how they are, and of things that are not as to how they are not."[9]

---

8 While we provide a number of citations to helpful works in the material that follows, it would be impossible to even scratch the surface of scholarship on the history of philosophy in this limited space. For readers interested in a scholarly source that aims to lay out the whole history, consider Anthony Kenny, *A New History of Western Philosophy* (Oxford: Oxford University Press, 2010). Will Durant's book is a very well-known, and much more accessible, narrative of this history: Will Durant, *The Story of Philosophy: The Lives and Opinions of the Greater Philosophers* (New York: Simon & Schuster, 2005).

9 For further reading, see Patricia Curd, "Presocratic Philosophy," *The Stanford Encyclopedia of Philosophy* (Fall 2020), ed. Edward N. Zalta, https://plato.stanford.edu/archives/sum2019/entries/presocratics/; Victor Ehrenberg, *From Solon to Socrates: Greek History and Civilization during the 6th and 5th Centuries BC* (London: Methuen, 1967), esp. 333–51; and G.B. Kerford, *The Sophistic Movement* (New York: Cambridge University Press, 1981).

All philosophers discussed so far may be characterized by the term "Pre-Socratic," a description that links them together thematically while also alluding to the monumental importance of Socrates in the history of philosophy. Socrates (469–399 BC) was an Athenian citizen who spent his whole life engaged in philosophizing. But in contrast with the "Pre-Socratics," he initiated a new method of conducting philosophy, if not a wholly new conception of philosophy itself. In Book Five of his *Tusculan Disputations*, the Roman statesman and philosopher Cicero famously referred to Socrates as "the first who brought down philosophy from the heavens, placed it in cities, introduced it to families, and obliged it to examine into life and morals, and good and evil."[10] In other words, these subjects central to the task of leadership – and to understanding leadership more fully – were squarely in the purview of this philosopher and the thinkers he influenced.

Socrates himself did not write any of his ideas down. What we know about his life and work is based on a limited number of primary sources: Aristophanes' comedy *Clouds*; the dialogues of Plato, all but one of which (the *Laws*) feature Socrates as a character; and a handful of Xenophon's writings. Given that the majority of these works are dramatic, it is a question whether the descriptions of Socrates' life were presented accurately or, instead, were crafted artfully. Xenophon's *Memorabilia*, for instance, recounts a number of the author's own recollections about the life and deeds of his teacher Socrates, memories that appear randomly presented but, in fact, deal with major themes such as piety, justice, and education.[11] For his part, Plato reports in a letter that the aim in writing his corpus was not to showcase his own voice, but rather to paint a picture of Socrates that rendered him beautiful and young.[12]

What is clear about the significance of Socrates, though, is that he is the founder of and enduring inspiration for the philosophic way of life. The aforementioned comment about Socrates from Cicero alludes to the so-called "Socratic turn," according to which he turned away from the study of natural science to focus instead on human nature, so as to pursue knowledge

---

10 Marcus Tullius Cicero, *Tusculan Disputations*, trans. J.E. King (Cambridge: Harvard University Press, 1971).
11 For a thoughtful reflection on how to apply the writings of Xenophon to leadership practice, see Brook Manville, "What If Xenophon Were Your Executive Coach?," *Forbes* (online), March 3, 2019, www.forbes.com/sites/brookmanville/2019/03/03/what-if-xenophon-were-your-executive-coach/#8f57b7222dcc.
12 This famous statement comes from Plato's "Second Letter." See Plato, *Epistles*, trans. Glenn Morrow (Indianapolis: Bobbs-Merrill, 1962), 198.

of the whole of nature in a new way.[13] Aristophanes' *Clouds* depicts a younger Socrates who conducts unorthodox scientific experiments, while Plato's dialogues *Parmenides* and *Phaedo* provide evidence for, and discussion of, his turn away from natural science toward the human things. The vast majority of texts featuring Socrates show a figure who engages in conversation with others in order to examine important subjects, most importantly human virtue or what constitutes true nobility and goodness.

We can say, then, that Socrates made major and influential contributions to the world that are rightfully thought of as leadership, insofar as he established philosophy as a worthwhile practice for humans and imparted on his students a passionate love for learning. He succeeded, with the help of his students, to such an extent that the example of his life is widely regarded as the standard for liberal education today. The context in which Socrates lived – the city of Athens, which was part of the larger Greek world – regarded philosophy and those devoted to it to be, at best, worthless for the aims of political life and, at worst, detrimental to the noble and good opinions that animated the city. Athens executed Socrates for suspicions that he was, in fact, dangerous to the city, but his powerful example of how one must engage in the quest for knowledge endures to this day.[14]

The greatest student of Socrates was Plato and the greatest student of Plato was Aristotle. Because these two titans of Greek philosophy are discussed at extensive length in this book's following chapters, we will refrain from discussing their significance here. But the wider Greek experience, as well as the Roman experience that came to dominate the world for many centuries, was not lacking in other philosophical traditions. Two of the most influential and intellectually stimulating were Stoicism and Epicureanism. Stoicism, founded in Athens in the 3rd Century BC by Zeno of Citium, claims some very famous historical adherents, such as the Roman philosopher Seneca (4 BC–65 AD) and Marcus Aurelius, the Emperor of Rome from 161 to 180 and a fascinating case study of the mutual influence of philosophy and leadership. Stoicism loosely traces its origins to Socrates and teaches that virtue, rooted in knowledge, is the key to right living. With this foundation

---

13 Catherine Zuckert provides an illuminating discussion of Plato's treatment of this change in Socrates' methods and objectives: see Catherine H. Zuckert, *Plato's Philosophers: The Coherence of the Dialogues* (Chicago: University of Chicago Press, 2009), esp. 180–214. See also Dustin Sebell, *The Socratic Turn: Knowledge of Good and Evil in an Age of Science* (Philadelphia: University of Pennsylvania Press, 2016).

14 Both Plato and Xenophon, Socrates' students, wrote dramatic depictions of the trial of their teacher Socrates in Athens. See Plato and Aristophanes, *Four Texts on Socrates*, rev. ed., trans. and ed. Thomas G. West and Grace Starry West (Ithaca, NY: Cornell University Press, 1989), 63–97; and Xenophon, *The Shorter Socratic Writings*, trans. and ed. Robert C. Bartlett (Ithaca: Cornell University Press, 1996), 9–17.

in virtue, the Stoic strives to be indifferent to pleasures and pains, and to shifting fortunes, without shameful complaints. Epicureanism came to be seen as a contrasting ideal to Stoicism, insofar as it teaches that pleasure is the chief good for humans. The founder of this doctrine was Epicurus (341–270 BC), a Greek philosopher who taught mainly in Athens, yet most of what we know of Epicureanism comes from the Roman poet Lucretius' magisterial work *On the Nature of Things* (ca. 60 BC), which lays out the doctrine in terms of both physics and ethics. For the Epicurean, pleasure in the sense of freedom from pain can be experienced by both the body and the mind. The key to happiness is tranquility, or a life lived without fears and other disturbances of one's inner existence experienced as pain.[15]

With the onset of Christianity and, perhaps more importantly, the official acceptance of Christianity into the Roman Empire as its religion, it seems accurate to say that the richness of the western philosophic experience was diminished, relative to its peak in the classical antiquity of Greece and Rome. That said, the very long period of western history roughly known as the Middle Ages was not without noteworthy examples of the pursuit of philosophic wisdom, many of which attempted to bring philosophy together with Christian teaching. Augustine (354–430) of Hippo, a city in North Africa in what is present-day Algeria, was one of the profoundest theologians of the early Church. But he has also been called "the first author to deal more or less comprehensively with the subject of civil society in the light of the new situation created by the emergence of [Christianity] and its encounter with philosophy in the Greco-Roman world."[16] The major work of political philosophy in which Augustine formulated these thoughts on civil society is called *City of God*. Other philosophers, writing much later, tasked themselves with interpreting Christian doctrine in the philosophical terms of Aristotle – and vice versa. Easily the most important thinker in this tradition is Thomas Aquinas (1225–1274), born in central Italy, whose *Summa Theologiae* methodically argues that Aristotle's ideas are consistent with Christian dogma. But Marsilius of Padua (ca. 1275–1342) also claims intellectual lineage from Aristotle. In his text *Defender of the Peace*, he makes an early argument that the principle of political sovereignty should rest in the whole body of citizens, rather than in the leaders of government.

As a consequence of the early 16th-century writings of the Florentine Niccolò Machiavelli, however, the history of western philosophy underwent a monumental transformation. Machiavelli, a firecracker of a thinker, shot

---

15 For further reading on Stoicism and Epicureanism, see Émile Bréhier, *The Hellenistic and Roman Age*, trans. Wade Baskin (Chicago: University of Chicago Press, 1965), esp. 23–94.
16 Ernest L. Fortin, "St. Augustine," in *History of Political Philosophy*, 3rd ed., ed. Leo Strauss and Joseph Cropsey (Chicago: University of Chicago Press, 1987), 176.

the first salvo against the ideas and ideals of classical antiquity and medieval Christianity. He thereby paved the way not simply for the Renaissance in Italy and throughout Europe, but also for the whole modern period of philosophy – a period in which we currently reside, half a millennium later, despite a multitude of developments over the centuries. Because Chapter 4 of this book is devoted to an extensive leadership-focused commentary on *The Prince*, we will refrain from saying much more about Machiavelli now. Suffice it to say, though, that Machiavelli's teaching contains the seeds from which so many modern concepts, not to mention the institutions of the modern world, would sprout and flourish, such as: the scientific method, the demand that theory have an effect on practice, the conquest of nature, secularization, liberal democracy, capitalist economics, and utilitarianism, just to name a handful.

For roughly two centuries after Machiavelli, philosophers worked out the scientific and political systems contained in the ideas of the great Florentine.[17] This period of early modern philosophy is also the origin of the intellectual movement known widely as the Enlightenment. Generally speaking, this movement promotes spreading arts and sciences to humanity so as to liberate ourselves from the forces that keep us down, with the ultimate aim of bettering human living conditions in an uncertain world. Key thinkers of this period made extraordinary advances in codifying the principles of the scientific method – largely the same principles that guide scientific research today. For instance, in his *Discourse on Method*, the French philosopher René Descartes (1596–1650) draws on mathematical ideas to explain how and why one should break problems down into their smallest manageable parts to build knowledge slowly and orderly, sticking as closely to the right process for scientific research as possible. Francis Bacon (1561–1626), who served in a leadership role as Lord Chancellor of England, wrote *The New Organon* with similar objectives in mind. Philosophers like Thomas Hobbes (1588–1679) and John Locke (1662–1704) were also focused on clarifying scientific principles, helping readers to see what can be known about the world surrounding them. Yet they are perhaps better known for their groundbreaking contributions to political and social philosophy, insofar as both were among the first to argue for the principles of government that would come to characterize liberal democracies. In the case of Locke, it is clear that his philosophical ideas would have a major impact on the practical world. His influence on the leaders of the American Revolution and

---

17 For a subtler and more developed discussion of the history of modern philosophy, consider Leo Strauss, "The Three Waves of Modernity," in *An Introduction to Political Philosophy: Ten Essays by Leo Strauss*, ed. Hilail Gildin (Detroit: Wayne State University Press, 1989), 81–98.

America's constitutional framers, for example, was profound. According to James Ceaser, Locke's *Second Treatise of Civil Government* was "the most widely read book in America in the 1770s, the Bible excepted."[18]

Of the many towering figures of philosophy writing in the 18th century, two thinkers stand the tallest: Jean-Jacques Rousseau (1712–1778) and Immanuel Kant (1724–1804). Indeed, to refer to the latter as a philosophical giant would be an understatement, as Kant is likely the most celebrated philosopher of the Enlightenment. While Kant's *Critique of Pure Reason* is his philosophical masterwork, containing his treatment of the faculty of reason, his article-length piece "What Is Enlightenment?" famously defends this broad intellectual movement as "the liberation of man from his self-imposed immaturity." Philosophy, in short, is the true means whereby humankind fulfills its humanity. Yet despite Kant's seminal role in the history of philosophy, the influence of Rousseau is both wider and deeper. In the middle of the 18th century, the writings of this philosopher from Geneva positioned the march of modern philosophy on a slightly different path and set it in motion.[19] Some scholars view Rousseau as a member of the Enlightenment, though others regard him as the founder of a so-called "Counter-Enlightenment," or a formal rejection of certain ideas from early modern philosophy.[20] In his *Discourse on the Sciences and Arts*, Rousseau appears to reject the ideal of the Enlightenment in arguing that the spread of science has been detrimental to humankind, even if it has been advantageous to particular individuals. And in his two most important texts, the *Discourse on the Origins and Foundations of Inequality among Men* and *Émile: or, On Education*, Rousseau set forth his fundamental idea that human beings are naturally good – a qualified refutation of the teaching on human nature one finds in the work of, say, Hobbes and Locke.

Much like with Machiavelli, it is possible to see Rousseau as the founder of many important intellectual and political movements, and he has one of the most colorful personal stories of anyone in the history of philosophy. He was a musician who invented a new form of musical notation. He was a botanist who left us a slew of important descriptive writings on plants. His electrifying writings on religion led to his banishment from Geneva and the

18 James Ceaser, "Between Us and the State of Nature," *Law & Liberty* (online source), June 23, 2020, accessed January 7, 2021, https://lawliberty.org/between-us-and-the-state-of-nature/.

19 Kant could have been influenced by Rousseau only in a very qualified manner – although one famous story relates that the only time Kant broke his daily habit of walking to and from his office in Königsberg (the original inspiration of the term "philosopher's walk") was when he received a copy of Rousseau's *Émile* and stayed at home with it, engrossed in the text.

20 See, for example, Graeme Garrard, *Rousseau's Counter-Enlightenment: A Republican Critique of the Philosophes* (Albany: State University of New York Press, 2003).

public burning of *Émile*. Some view Rousseau as the intellectual prophet of the French Revolution – although the arguments for his leadership in this regard are disputed. He is, finally, the founder of the modern political left, environmentalism, romanticism, transcendentalism, the cult of compassion, the notion of public sincerity and authenticity as a human ideal, and modern anthropology, among many other things.[21]

Many philosophers working in the intellectual space carved out by Rousseau latched on to the Genevan's emphasis on history, the governing force for human relations, as the polestar for philosophic speculation. For instance, Georg Hegel (1770–1831) developed a comprehensive philosophy of history as the development of individual consciousness, or "spirit." For Hegel, history moves forward in stages, where the dominant ideal in human culture, that is, "thesis," comes into a struggle with a contrary ideal, that is, "antithesis," and through this conflict emerges a new ideal, that is, "synthesis." The process moves forward from there, creating ever new social conditions. Hegel conceives of an end to this historical progress, concluding in the absolute freedom of the spirit. Karl Marx (1818–1883) famously took up Hegel's theory of history and developed the concept of historical materialism, according to which history moves in a similar manner, although the material conditions of the mode of production, rather than ideals, drive the process. As is well known, Marx is the key intellectual support for the political systems of socialism and communism. He argued that the class of workers must necessarily engage in a struggle with the owners of production in the capitalist political economy, overthrowing them eventually and leaving the whole collectivity as owners of the mode of production. It may not be a stretch to suggest that Marx, more than anyone in the history of philosophy, conceives of the role of the theorist to be reforming the practical world. As he famously said in his *Theses on Feuerbach* (#11), the "philosophers have only *interpreted* the world in various ways; the point is, to *change* it."[22]

Friedrich Nietzsche (1844–1900) lived and wrote in the late 19th century, but his writings and thought paved the way for philosophic speculation through the present day. A classical philologist by professional training,

21 Those eager to learn more about Jean-Jacques Rousseau should consult the authoritative three-volume history of his life and work by Maurice Cranston. Maurice Cranston, *Jean-Jacques: The Early Life and Work of Jean-Jacques Rousseau, 1712–1754* (Chicago: University of Chicago Press, 1991); Maurice Cranston, *The Noble Savage: Jean-Jacques Rousseau, 1754–1762* (Chicago: University of Chicago Press, 1999); and Maurice Cranston, *The Solitary Self: Jean-Jacques Rousseau in Exile and Adversity* (Chicago: University of Chicago Press, 1999).

22 Karl Marx, *Selected Writings*, ed. Lawrence H. Simon (Indianapolis: Hackett, 1994), 101, (emphasis in original).

Nietzsche moved in his career to explore a wide array of ideas, such as the nature of the tragic outlook and the fundamental role of power in and for all things. In his texts *Beyond Good and Evil* and *On the Genealogy of Morals*, he attempts to uncover the true nature of moral categories. Nietzsche believed that philosophers were legislators of values. In other words, the job of philosophy was to artistically establish the major ideals around which civilizations revolve. Martin Heidegger (1889–1976), the most influential philosopher of the 20th century and precursor to all postmodern thought, changed the way we think about philosophy, literature, art, and history. His philosophy can be summed up in this way: he sought to destroy Western metaphysics to elicit an ontology of Being. In his *magnum opus, Being and Time* (1927), Heidegger begins this project through an existential analysis of "Dasein," the being that is aware of its being, or the human being. He attracted an ardent following of talented students who went on to prominent careers as philosophers such as Hannah Arendt, Karl Löwith, and Herbert Marcuse. Later in his career, Heidegger turned to the subjects of technology, language, and art.[23]

The influence of both Nietzsche and Heidegger on postmodern thought cannot be understated.[24] Michel Foucault, the philosopher of power relations and a self-styled neo-Nietzschean, is now a canonical figure in gender-queer theory, critical race theory, and postmodern history. Meanwhile, Jacques Lacan developed his early psychoanalytic theory based on Heidegger's philosophy. Jacques Derrida, indebted to Lacan and Heidegger, coined his famous term *la difference*, which is now a staple of literary criticism in American universities.

Why Plato, Aristotle, and Machiavelli? The plan for the book

Considering the preceding discussion, it should be clear that there is a host of philosophers and their texts that we might have chosen to explore in this book. Yet, out of all of the possibilities, we have selected Plato's *Republic*, Aristotle's *Nicomachean Ethics*, and Machiavelli's *The Prince*. Why these three?

---

23 For a lucid discussion of Heidegger's philosophy that is sensitive to the theme of leadership, see Hans Pedersen, "Heidegger on Authenticity: The Prospect of Owning One's Existence," in *Leadership and the Unmasking of Authenticity: The Philosophy of Self-Knowledge and Deception*, ed. Brent Edwin Cusher and Mark A. Menaldo (Northampton, UK: Edward Elgar, 2018), 57–74.

24 Consider Thomas L. Pangle, *The Ennobling of Democracy: The Challenge of the Postmodern Age* (Baltimore, MD: The Johns Hopkins University Press, 1992), esp. 34–47.

The simplest answer to this question is that we sought to interpret the texts that are most closely connected with the most important themes in leadership. When scholars turn to philosophy for insights into leadership, often Plato, Aristotle, and Machiavelli's names are first to come up on their radar.[25] And the influence of each thinker was both profound and wide-ranging. The two classical Greeks are monumentally important, in no small part, because they did their intellectual work when philosophy was relatively new. Their ideas seem fresh and accessible – despite having been written down some 2,500 years ago. For his part, Machiavelli was not just a theorist of leadership but was himself an immensely influential leader. As we indicated, modern philosophy, politics, and culture are what they are largely because the Florentine thought what he thought and wrote what he wrote. It seems natural, then, that these three philosophers should enjoy pride of place. Finally, each text examined in our book provides a vehicle for examining, in turn, an essential topic: the role of philosophical learning in and for leadership; character ethics; and the concept of moral flexibility as a way of leading. We expected that treating these three philosophers' texts, carefully and comprehensively, would result in a richly diverse analysis of leadership.

Chapter 2 is devoted to Plato's *Republic*, which recounts a conversation about justice where Socrates is the leading player. More than two millennia after his life and famous death in Athens, Socrates is still the standard for philosophy in its original and truest sense – that is, the love of wisdom and the life devoted to its pursuit. Plato's entire corpus is dedicated to articulating and defending the Socratic life, yet it is in the *Republic* where one finds the best analysis of what philosophy means and what philosophic education demands. This chapter interprets the *Republic* as showing not only what philosophers do in their inquiries but also the kind of human being philosophers must be. Socrates seems to say that there can be no improvement in communities unless philosophers take the reins in public leadership. Still, based on our interpretation of the *Republic*'s famous allegory of the cave, the truer lesson for leadership is that philosophers are leaders insofar as they play a role in educating others to a philosophic life. We conclude this chapter with a brief recounting of the story of Dion of Syracuse, a great friend of Plato who attempted – unsuccessfully, as the history goes – to bring philosophic learning to bear on the governance of his native city.

---

25 It is telling that J. Thomas Wren, in his classic and widely read compilation of readings on leadership, has chosen to include brief selections from these three authors as his only selections from philosophy (though Wren has included a passage from Aristotle's *The Politics*, not the *Nicomachean Ethics*). See J. Thomas Wren, ed., *The Leader's Companion: Insights on Leadership through the Ages* (New York: The Free Press, 1995), 60–8.

Aristotle's *Nicomachean Ethics* comes into focus in Chapter 3. It is a truism to say that character matters – as a general rule for life and as a principle of leadership. But how does it matter, and how does one develop an appropriate character? The *Ethics* provides illuminating and thorough answers to these questions, perhaps the most illuminating answers available to us. Our chapter interprets Aristotle's thoughts on how the deliberate development of moral virtue, through habituation toward virtuous means, is the cornerstone of an individual's character formation. We hope that readers will find this chapter particularly useful, because Aristotle's examination of moral excellence is the pillar of two common ideas that are held about leadership: first, leadership excellence is both desirable and learnable; and second, becoming one's best self is something in one's control. Rather than providing a full treatment of Aristotle's whole book, however, we concentrate on the virtue of greatness of soul, *megalopsychia*, specifically, showing that this settled disposition toward the greatest honors is relevant to how we understand and speak about leadership today. As with Chapter 2, we close this one out with a discussion of a famous leader who was part of Aristotle's world: Alexander the Great, Aristotle's student and ruler of an enormous empire.

Niccolò Machiavelli's ideas, which are the subject of Chapter 4, are instructive for leaders who find themselves in situations that offer little guidance in the form of pre-existing rules and norms. For Machiavelli, as we see in *The Prince*, these are the princes who found altogether new principalities. Princes are the head not only of government but of the political culture as well. Machiavelli's presentation of leadership is situational. Leaders must learn how to use moral characteristics as circumstances arise, for the sake of acquiring and aggrandizing their dominions. In short, leaders will revert to anything to become successful. As this chapter shows, Machiavelli was the first to understand the ethical dilemma of the entrepreneur, the one who undertakes and manages high-stake operations that affect many people. We portray these ideas by providing some commentary on Cesare Borgia's experiences, the son of Pope Alexander VI and an acquaintance of Machiavelli. While it would be a stretch to call Borgia a perfect Machiavellian prince, he was a major political player in Italy. He embodied most of Machiavelli's ideas in and for leadership. As we shall see, under these circumstances just how ethical a leader is in his dealings with others is of grave concern.

Our book concludes with three case studies from much more recent history to illustrate the principles of our philosophers in their real-world application. Corresponding with Plato's *Republic*, we look at the life and leadership of Bill Gates, founder of Microsoft Corporation and key player in The Bill and Melinda Gates Foundation. Nelson Mandela, the anti-apartheid revolutionary in South Africa and former president of his home country, helps us see the dimensions of Aristotle's great-souled man more precisely. And our suspicion that Al Dunlap, former CEO of several US companies, would bring the principles of Machiavellian leadership into sharp relief was most definitely borne out by our research. In presenting these three examples, we do not argue, in any way, that there is a perfect correspondence between the philosophic text, on the one hand, and the real-world example of the case study, on the other. We do not intend to say, for instance, that Mandela was the realization of the perfect great-souled leader, precisely along the lines of Aristotle's famous model from the *Ethics*. But we are confident that the points of connection between the philosophic ideas and the real-world examples can illuminate each other in interesting ways. In Chapter 5, we present these case studies straightforwardly and without any comments to introduce or conclude the chapter as a whole. We intend to let the case studies speak for themselves and allow the reader to decide, for himself or herself, whether and to what degree they embody the philosophic ideas discussed.

Bibliography

Audi, Robert. *Epistemology: A Contemporary Introduction to the Theory of Knowledge*. 3rd ed. New York: Routledge, 2010.

———. "The Field of Philosophy: Philosophy: A Brief Guide for Undergraduates." *The American Philosophical Association*, 2017. www.apaonline.org/page/undergraduates.

Bréhier, Émile. *The Hellenistic and Roman Age*. Translated by Wade Baskin. Chicago: University of Chicago Press, 1965.

Ceaser, James. "Between Us and the State of Nature." *Law & Liberty*, June 23, 2020. https://lawliberty.org/between-us-and-the-state-of-nature/.

Cicero, Marcus Tullius. *Tusculan Disputations*. Translated by J.E. King. Cambridge: Harvard University Press, 1971.

Ciulla, Joanne B., ed. *Ethics, the Heart of Leadership*. 2nd ed. Westport, CT: Praeger, 2004.

Cranston, Maurice. *Jean-Jacques: The Early Life and Work of Jean-Jacques Rousseau, 1712–1754*. Chicago: University of Chicago Press, 1991.

———. *The Noble Savage: Jean-Jacques Rousseau, 1754–1762*. Chicago: University of Chicago Press, 1999.

———. *The Solitary Self: Jean-Jacques Rousseau in Exile and Adversity*. Chicago: University of Chicago Press, 1999.

Curd, Patricia. "Presocratic Philosophy." *The Stanford Encyclopedia of Philosophy* (Fall 2020 Edition). Edited by Edward N. Zalta. https://plato.stanford.edu/archives/fall2020/entries/presocratics/.

Cusher, Brent Edwin, and Mark A. Menaldo, eds. *Leadership and the Unmasking of Authenticity: The Philosophy of Self-Knowledge and Deception*. Northampton, UK: Edward Elgar, 2018.

Durant, Will. *The Story of Philosophy: The Lives and Opinions of the Greater Philosophers*. New York: Simon and Schuster, 2005.

Ehrenberg, Victor. *From Solon to Socrates: Greek History and Civilization during the 6th and 5th Centuries BC*. London: Methuen, 1967.

Elshtain, Jean Bethke. "Leadership and the Humanities." In *Leadership and the Liberal Arts: Achieving the Promise of a Liberal Education*, edited by J. Thomas Wren, Ronald E. Riggio, and Michael A. Genovese, 117–25. New York: Palgrave Macmillan, 2009.

Flanigan, Jessica. "Philosophical Methodology and Leadership Ethics." *Leadership* 14, no. 6 (2018): 707–30.

Fortin, Ernest L. "St. Augustine." In *History of Political Philosophy*, 3rd ed., edited by Leo Strauss and Joseph Cropsey, 176–205. Chicago: University of Chicago Press, 1987.

Gardiner, Rita. "Gender, Authenticity, and Leadership: Thinking with Arendt." *Leadership* 12, no. 5 (2016): 632–37.

Garrard, Graeme. *Rousseau's Counter-Enlightenment: A Republican Critique of the Philosophes*. Albany: State University of New York Press, 2003.

Gensler, Harry J. *Ethics: A Contemporary Introduction*. 3rd ed. New York: Routledge, 2017.

Harter, Nathan W. *Foucault on Leadership*. New York: Routledge, 2016.

Kenny, Anthony. *A New History of Western Philosophy*. Oxford: Oxford University Press, 2010.

Keohane, Nannerl O. *Thinking about Leadership*. Princeton, NJ: Princeton University Press, 2012.

Kerford, G.B. *The Sophistic Movement*. New York: Cambridge University Press, 1981.

Lawler, John, and Ian Ashman. "Theorizing Leadership Authenticity: A Sartrean Perspective." *Leadership* 8, no. 4 (2012): 327–44.

Loux, Michael J., and Thomas M. Crisp. *Metaphysics: A Contemporary Introduction*. 4th ed. New York: Routledge, 2017.

Manville, Brook. "What If Xenophon Were Your Executive Coach?" *Forbes*, March 3, 2019. www.forbes.com/sites/brookmanville/2019/03/03/what-if-xenophon-were-your-executive-coach/#8f57b7222dcc.

Marturano, Antonio, J. Thomas Wren, and Michael Harvey. "Editorial: The Making of Leadership and the Humanities." *Leadership and the Humanities* 1, no. 1 (2013): 1–5.

Marx, Karl. *Selected Writings*. Edited by Lawrence H. Simon. Indianapolis: Hackett, 1994.

Pangle, Thomas L. *The Ennobling of Democracy: The Challenge of the Postmodern Age*. Baltimore: The Johns Hopkins University Press, 1992.

Pedersen, Hans. "Heidegger on Authenticity: The Prospect of Owning One's Existence." In *Leadership and the Unmasking of Authenticity: The Philosophy of Self-Knowledge and Deception*, edited by Brent Edwin Cusher and Mark A. Menaldo, 57–74. Northampton, UK: Edward Elgar, 2018.

Plato. *Epistles*. Translated by Glenn Morrow. Indianapolis: Bobbs-Merrill, 1962.

Plato, and Aristophanes. *Four Texts on Socrates.* Rev. ed. Edited and Translated by Thomas G. West and Grace Starry West. Ithaca, NY: Cornell University Press, 1989.

Price, Terry L. *Leadership and the Ethics of Influence.* New York: Routledge, 2020.

———. *Understanding Ethical Failures in Leadership.* New York: Cambridge University Press, 2006.

Schwitzgebel, Eric. "What Kinds of Universities Lack Philosophy Departments? Some Data." *Daily Nous,* March 22, 2017. http://dailynous.com/2017/03/22/kinds-universities-lack-philosophy-departments-data-guest-post-eric-schwitzgebel/.

Sebell, Dustin. *The Socratic Turn: Knowledge of Good and Evil in an Age of Science.* Philadelphia: University of Pennsylvania Press, 2016.

Sison, Alejo José G. *The Moral Capital of Leaders: Why Virtue Matters.* Northampton, UK: Edward Elgar, 2004.

Strauss, Leo. "The Three Waves of Modernity." In *An Introduction to Political Philosophy: Ten Essays by Leo Strauss,* edited by Hilail Gildin, 81–98. Detroit: Wayne State University Press, 1989.

Strauss, Leo, and Joseph Cropsey, eds. *History of Political Philosophy.* 3rd ed. Chicago: University of Chicago Press, 1987.

Wren, J. Thomas, ed. *The Leader's Companion: Insights on Leadership through the Ages.* New York: The Free Press, 1995.

Xenophon. *The Shorter Socratic Writings.* Translated and Edited by Robert C. Bartlett. Ithaca: Cornell University Press, 1996.

Zuckert, Catherine H. *Plato's Philosophers: The Coherence of the Dialogues.* Chicago: University of Chicago Press, 2009.

2 Plato

Wisdom for leadership and philosophy as leadership

As we have illustrated in Chapter 1, those looking for insight about leadership through the lens of philosophy would be well served to begin with Socrates. In taking this step, however, one quickly comes to see how essential the life and writings of Plato (ca. 429–347 BC), the greatest student of Socrates, are to this pursuit. It is the Heraclean effort of Plato to describe and interpret his teacher in writing that serves as the best foundation on which Socrates' reputation rests. Plato was an Athenian who came from an aristocratic family of very high status, the kind of family whose sons could have expected to follow a resplendent career of political and military leadership for Athens. That Plato decided to follow Socrates in the way of philosophy instead has been regarded by some as something of a coup with world-historical significance. The 19th-century German philosopher Friedrich Nietzsche, for instance, has remarked that the noble character of Plato was corrupted by Socrates and, furthermore, that the primary task of Plato's life was to creatively interpret Socrates in line with his own nobility.[1] Regardless of how one chooses to view the significance of Plato's relationship with his teacher, his first and most important contribution to our understanding of leadership is to have spread the word about the Socratic life to the wider world, including posterity, through artful writing.

Now, it is true that Plato's significance for leadership is not limited to his task to promote philosophy as a worthwhile pursuit. Historians know that Plato himself was responsible for several projects for which he may be rightfully called a leader. During his lifetime, he founded and led a successful school, located approximately one mile from Athens in a grove called *Akademeia*.[2] Plato also played some ambiguous role as an advisor to

---

1 Consider, e.g., Friedrich Nietzsche, *Beyond Good and Evil: Prelude to a Philosophy of the Future*, trans. Walter Kaufmann (New York: Vintage Books, 1989), 2.

2 For more information on Plato's school, see Paul Kalligas, Chloe Balla, Effie Baziotopoulou-Valavani, and Vassilis Karasmanis, eds., *Plato's Academy: Its Workings and Its History* (Cambridge: Cambridge University Press, 2020).

political leaders when he visited Syracuse, a city on Sicily, several times in the middle of his life. He was first invited to Syracuse by the city's tyrant Dionysius I, who had been encouraged to do so by Dion, a Syracusan nobleman interested in philosophy. Plato recounts his several experiences on Sicily in a series of letters.[3] We will return to these themes, and specifically the leadership of Dion, later in this chapter.

Yet, despite these critical experiences in Plato's life, one must search instead the writings to discover his essential thoughts about leadership, for these are the fertile field left to posterity in which the philosopher rooted his ideas. As we have noted, the overwhelming majority of Platonic writings concern Socrates and the philosophic way of life to which he led his students. There are 35 dialogues – that is, dramatic texts that present conversations between different characters – attributed to Plato and 34 of these feature Socrates in some manner. Of the entire collection, it is the *Republic* that contains the best analysis of what philosophy means and what philosophic education requires. Among the most celebrated philosophic texts ever written, and arguably the most profound, Plato's *Republic* elaborates a human type that has come to be known as the "philosopher-king," a figure that many scholars identify as Plato's answer to the question of the best leader.[4] Socrates famously says in this text that unless

> the philosophers rule as kings or those now called kings and chiefs genuinely and adequately philosophize, and political power and philosophy coincide in the same place . . . there is no rest from ills for the cities . . . nor I think for human kind.
>
> (473c–d)[5]

In this chapter, we demonstrate the benefits of knowing and reflecting on Plato's *Republic* for a rich understanding of leadership. Considering Socrates' statement on the confluence of "political power and philosophy,"

---

3 Plato, *Epistles*, trans. Glenn Morrow (Indianapolis: Bobbs-Merrill, 1962), esp. 215–57. See also Joanne B. Ciulla, "Plato (c. 428-c. 348 BCE)," in *Encyclopedia of Leadership*, ed. George R. Goethels, Georgia J. Sorenson, and James MacGregor Burns (Thousand Oaks, CA: SAGE, 2004), 1202–3.

4 See, *inter alia*, Ciulla, "Plato (c. 428-c. 348 BCE)"; Thomas E. Cronin and Michael A. Genovese, *Leadership Matters: Unleashing the Power of Paradox* (Boulder, CO: Paradigm Publishers, 2012), 77, 82–4; T. Takala, "Plato on Leadership," *Journal of Business Ethics* 17 (1998): 792; and J. Thomas Wren, ed., *The Leader's Companion: Insights on Leadership through the Ages* (New York: The Free Press, 1995), 60–4.

5 All citations to Plato's *Republic* will be made in parentheses in the text according to the standard Stephanus numbers accessible in all editions of Plato's work. We have taken direct quotations from the *Republic* from the following translation: Allan Bloom, *The Republic of Plato*, 2nd ed. (New York: Basic Books, 1968).

we aim to clarify what the *Republic* teaches us about both philosophy as a human pursuit and the identity of the philosopher, the individual most in line with justice. Plato argues that the possession of a certain kind of knowledge – or, stated more precisely, an attitude toward acquiring and possessing knowledge – is the essential element of good leadership. Accordingly, Plato's philosophic text is particularly useful for helping us see the connections between leadership and education, broadly understood. As we shall see by looking more closely at the famous allegory of the cave, Socrates and his interlocutors in the *Republic* argue that philosophers are leaders insofar as they fulfill a role in educating others to a philosophic life. This idea does not mean that to lead well, one must truly become a philosopher, thereby devoting one's entire life to theoretical contemplation. Rather, as we shall discuss throughout this chapter, and as shall become clear with reference to the example of Bill Gates in Chapter 5, Plato's notion that the good life is open to the need for examination of the most important things has clear implications for leadership as we understand it today.

The *Republic* of Plato: structure and themes

The *Republic* is a narrated dialogue, which is a literary form that presents a recitation of events delivered by one character.[6] In this case, that character is Socrates, and he recounts a conversation in which he took part during the previous day in the Piraeus, the port of Athens. A citizen of Athens, Socrates had traveled to the Piraeus with Glaucon, which is the name of one of Plato's real-life brothers. The two men found themselves at the home of Cephalus, a prosperous resident-alien in Athens originally from Syracuse. Most of the other participants in the conversation at Cephalus' home are young men, such as Polemarchus, the son of Cephalus, and Adeimantus, who happens to be another brother of Plato. The famous sophist Thrasymachus, a teacher of rhetoric looking to sell his services to students, is also in attendance. Yet, despite the presence of these characters, the vast majority of the conversation, spanning an entire night, takes place between Socrates, Glaucon, and Adeimantus.

Plato's text is titled, in the original Greek, *Politeia*. The reason why English speakers refer to this dialogue as the *Republic* is that Cicero, the famous Roman statesman and philosopher, did so himself. Cicero wrote a dialogue in Latin that was intended to correspond to this one – to be "an homage" in

---

6 See Margalit Finkelberg, *The Gatekeeper: Narrative Voice in Plato's Dialogues* (Leiden, NLD: Brill, 2019), esp. 34–8. These dialogues are contrasted by "performed dialogues," which include speeches of several characters and could, in theory, be performed dramatically.

some ways to Plato's[7] – and he called it *De re publica*, literally "on the public thing" or the Commonwealth. In Greek, however, *Politeia* had a more extensive range of meaning. It could be what we would think of as a republic, that is, a self-governing community with its corresponding leadership and citizenship structure. It could have been, by contrast, a form of government where everyone was ruled by the few or by the many, that is, what we might think of as a kind of despotism. The best direct translation for the word *Politeia* is "regime," which is a condition of organized human life having a specific character based on the ordering of its parts. For instance, the elements of the liberal democratic regime of the United States – such as its political offices, individual leaders and followers, institutions, cultural values, etc. – are arranged in such a manner to promote the goods of freedom and equality, in addition to the life most in line with those goods. Maybe the best way to think about *Politeia*, then, is to refer to something comprehensive like one's way of life. This, in short, is the title of Plato's dialogue, and provides a clue into its general subject.[8]

Yet the particular subject of the conversation of the *Republic*, and the means by which the artful Plato has his characters fill out their examination of the regime, is justice.[9] Recognizing justice as the most crucial good for human beings early in the conversation, in Book One, the speakers consider several definitions of justice. Some of these are conventional, others radical – yet they all are refuted to some degree by Socrates. The brothers Glaucon and Adeimantus, however, seize the reins at the opening of Book Two and shift the parameters of the discussion completely. No longer are they primarily interested in what justice is, but rather whether justice is good for the individual (357a). What does it mean to have justice in one's soul? What regime produces it most effectively? Is justice truly the greatest good for humans, or is it a sham that benefits those who can be successfully wicked? Is justice truly conducive to happiness? These questions are in play for the rest of the conversation until it wraps up in the early morning light.

We should pause for a moment to recognize a point that is nothing if not straightforward. When we aspire to know about leadership such that we hope to see it practiced in the world, what we mean is good leadership, moral or ethical leadership, or leadership for the right ends. We humans naturally hope for leaders, in whatever capacity they may serve (i.e., politics, society,

---

7 Jonathan Powell and Niall Rudd, "Introduction," in Cicero, *The Republic and The Laws*, trans. Niall Rudd (Oxford: Oxford University Press, 1998), xvi.

8 For an illuminating discussion of the full meaning of *Politeia*, see Leo Strauss, *Natural Right and History* (Chicago: University of Chicago Press, 1965), 135–9.

9 The subtitle commonly associated with *Republic* is "On the Just" – though scholars believe that this subtitle was not Plato's. Rather, it was added by a later editor.

business, religion, culture), to operate in accordance with justice and to do things that make their organizations, perhaps even their followers, more just. Now, it is unfortunately beyond the scope of this chapter to review every significant opinion about justice from Plato's dialogue, beyond what we will discuss in the following. But to the degree that Plato's *Republic* explores the meaning and nature of justice, this essential quality of human relationships, the text brightly illuminates matters essential to leadership.[10]

In order to determine whether justice truly is good for the individual, Socrates proposes to construct a city in speech. Assuming that there is justice both in an individual human being and in a city as a whole, he says that "perhaps there would be more justice in the bigger and it would be easier to observe closely" (368e). Glaucon, unable to tolerate the thought of a simple city that exists only to satisfy the basic needs of its citizens, demands at the outset that the city must provide some of the relishes of life to her citizens (372c–e). From here, the city grows in conversation to its maturity. Plato's *Republic* is famous for the creation of this city – presented as the good and just political order[11] – and the several elements that comprise it. There will be three classes of citizens in the perfectly just city: (1) the rulers; (2) a class auxiliary to the rulers that will defend the city from external threats; and (3) the money-making class of people. Socrates explains that each class will be the province of a particular kind of human virtue, or excellence. If one examines the rulers, those who have the best judgment for leading the city, one will see wisdom on display. The auxiliary class demonstrates courage. And the common run of people in the money-making class are supposed to embody moderation. Justice, the fourth of the cardinal virtues, is the proper and harmonious relationship of all classes working together, each doing its part. "Justice," Socrates finally says, "is the minding of one's own business and not being a busybody" (433a–b).

Yet we recall that Socrates had proposed to build the city in speech, not to draft a blueprint for the best political regime – some community one may encounter anyplace in the real world – but rather as a heuristic device for exploring the significance of justice in an individual human soul. Accordingly, the interlocutors explore how the relationship between the different

---

10 Studies that are particularly sensitive to the connection between Plato's *Republic* and leadership ethics are: David C. Bauman, "Plato on Virtuous Leadership: An Ancient Model for Modern Business," *Business Ethics Quarterly* 28, no. 3 (2018): 251–74; Jessica Flannigan, "Philosophical Methodology and Leadership Ethics," *Leadership* 14, no 6 (2018): 716–17; and Terry L. Price, *Leadership Ethics: An Introduction* (New York: Cambridge University Press, 2008), 68–73.

11 Socrates also refers to this constructed city at one place in the dialogue (527c) as *kallipolis*, "beautiful city."

classes of the city sheds light on the different parts of a human soul and their relationship to one another. Indeed, Socrates assumes here that the four virtues identified in the discussion (wisdom, courage, moderation, and justice) illuminate the nature of the human soul because they are each located in its different parts. Given that there are three classes in the city, there will be three classes in the soul. This is a model of human psychology that scholars have referred to as "the tri-partite soul."[12] Just as one finds wisdom in the class of rulers, one finds wisdom in reason, the part of the soul that thinks and calculates things. Spiritedness, corresponding to the auxiliary class, is the wellspring of courage, and it represents the quality in us that passionately stands up in defense of our own. Finally, appetite is the part of the soul that desires things, but in particular the lower kinds of pleasures like those of "nourishment [i.e., food and drink] and generation [i.e., sex] and all their kin" (436a). This part would naturally seem to be the home of moderation, because the task of this virtue is to provide a check on our pursuit of pleasure. Justice, finally, is the harmonious relationship of these three parts, each doing the job it is supposed to do for a human being. In other words, the just individual is the one whose reason, with the assistance of spiritedness, rules the appetites in a stable fashion.

This apparent breakthrough in the development of the city – that is, the discovery of justice – is not nearly the end of the story, though. Despite Socrates wanting to continue exploring the parallel between city and soul, Polemarchus and Thrasymachus stage an intervention in the conversation, asking Socrates to expand on a comment he had made previously that "as for women and children, the things of friends will be in common" (449c; cf. 423e). Is the family not the sturdy building block of the mature political community – and if so, what could Socrates mean by his comment? In his response, which sets forth the digression lasting for most of the rest of the conversation, Socrates expounds on three themes that, he says, would seem "ridiculous" compared with the habitual way that political leadership works in the real world (452a). Indeed, he argues that the founders of this city in speech would have to institute three radical innovations for the ideal regime to come into being and for it to function properly. First, this city would require a common program of education for both men and women, including physical education, to open the ruling class to both women and men (see 452a–457b). Second, among the guardian class, there would have to be a communism of women and children – that is, a formal and meticulously

---

12 For a source that thoroughly explains this tripartition of the soul, and also explores ways in which Plato wants us to understand this model as being more complicated than it first appears, consider Laurence D. Cooper, "Beyond the Tripartite Soul: The Dynamic Psychology of the *Republic*," *Review of Politics* 63, no. 2 (2001): 341–72.

regulated policy of eugenics whereby men and women make children solely for the benefit of the city, and no children identify themselves with their biological parents (see 457d–471e).[13] Third, and the reform to which Socrates refers as "the biggest and most difficult" (472a), this city would have to be ruled by philosophers as kings.

Leadership as philosophy: philosophers as kings and otherwise

The assertion that philosophers are the truest leaders – in other words, that the good society requires philosophers to rule as kings – is, of course, not especially clear or useful in itself. It begs a number of very obvious questions, most importantly: who is a philosopher and what is philosophy? And while the general aim of our book is to examine philosophic texts to arrive at a better understanding of leadership, it should be noted that of the three texts discussed at length, only Plato's *Republic* presents a substantial, focused, and detailed examination of the philosopher. One is tempted to say that Socrates engages in the conversation of this dialogue, to the extent that he does, not primarily so that he can establish a practical outline for healthy political life, but rather so that he can identify the philosopher as the most just individual and can, in the process, teach Glaucon and Adeimantus something about the nature of philosophy. After all, these young men are the sort who could be ambitious for a public leadership role in the city of Athens and who therefore may benefit from learning more about philosophy. And Socrates surely knows that he is competing for their attention with the likes of the sophist Thrasymachus, who had earlier made the shocking assertion that the best human life is that of the successful tyrant – the one powerfully committed to injustice on the largest scale (343b–344d). Leadership as the life of philosophy could provide a sturdy counterweight to that alarming argument, one which portends terrible injustices in the real world.

What, then, is a philosopher, according to Plato's *Republic*? At this point in the dialogue, Socrates suggests that one reason why people view philosophers with suspicion in public life is that they do not adequately understand what philosophers are. He begins to explain his meaning here by calling attention to the psychological phenomenon of *eros*. Translated plainly as "love," *eros* is a force of soul that arises in response to a feeling

---

13 For very insightful interpretations of these two reforms, consult Steven Forde, "Gender and Justice in Plato," *American Political Science Review* 91, no. 3 (1997): 657–70; James Nendza, "Nature and Convention in Book V of the *Republic*," *Canadian Journal of Political Science* 21, no. 2 (1988): 331–57; and Arlene W. Saxonhouse, "The Philosopher and the Female in the Political Thought of Plato," *Political Theory* 4, no. 2 (1976): 195–212.

of incompleteness. It directs energy toward finding and acquiring the thing that one lacks.[14] The nature of this passion is to be in love not just with a particular instance of a thing, but with all of the thing. Lovers of wine, for example, will take "delight in every kind of wine, and on every pretext" (475a). And along these terms, Socrates explains that a philosopher is a lover of wisdom: "the one who is willing to taste every kind of learning with gusto, and who approaches learning with delight, and is insatiable, we shall justly assert to be a philosopher" (475c).[15] These individuals are in love with the truth, or at least with the sight of it. In short, philosophers find ideas to be delightful.

It is impossible to grasp what philosophy truly is, according to Socrates, without understanding the distinction between knowledge, opinion, and ignorance, as these are three of the essential categories related to thinking. Knowledge refers to and is dependent on "the things that are." One can know, in other words, the things that correspond to reality. By contrast, ignorance lacks this correspondence and is therefore the precise opposite condition of knowledge. Ignorance is dependent on "the things that are not" and refers to a kind of thinking that does not match with reality. Opinion, finally, is the condition that exists in the space between knowledge and ignorance. Hence, it depends somehow on the things that are, on one hand, and the things that are not, on the other, combining these opposites in the human soul at the same time. Socrates here explains that the knower differs from the individual who merely opines in the same way that a wakeful person differs from one who is asleep and dreaming. Opinion is like dreaming, "whether one is asleep or awake," which consists "in believing a likeness of something to be not a likeness, but rather the thing itself to which it is like" (476c). Philosophers, in short, are the human beings who are most awake to the nature of the world as it is. They, "rather than lovers of opinion," Socrates clarifies, are "those who delight in each thing that is itself" (480a). The philosopher least of all humans suffers from the overwhelming delusions that make us convinced in the reality of ideas that are either blatant falsehoods or problematic in some decisive way.

One memorable element of Socrates' description of philosophers is their rarity, perhaps to an extreme degree. Indeed, reflecting on these passages of the *Republic*, it would be hard not to conclude that, in Socrates' view, most

---

14 Plato's dialogue that is centrally concerned with the nature of *eros* is the *Symposium*: see Plato, *Symposium*, trans. Seth Benardete (Chicago: University of Chicago Press, 2001). Consider also Allan Bloom, *Love and Friendship* (New York: Simon and Schuster, 1993), 13–33.

15 As we noted in Chapter One, the Greek world *philosophia* combines two words meaning "love" (*philia*) and "wisdom" (*sophia*).

human beings sleep their lives away, so to speak, passionately clinging to certain opinions about the world that do not make rational sense, despite how comforting to us they may be.[16] There is a long, well-established tradition in the study of leadership to highlight the various attributes of leaders that correlate with effectiveness. Sometimes labeled "the trait approach," these theories generally identify the physical and psychological traits, elements of personality, and other competencies that one tends to find in effective leaders.[17] Socrates in the *Republic*, it would seem, operates in a comparable way to these more contemporary theorists, in that he delineates the attributes of a young soul truly capable of philosophy. He explains that one "could never adequately pursue" philosophy "if he were not by nature a rememberer, a good learner, magnificent, charming, and a friend and kinsman of truth, justice, courage, and moderation" (487a). In other words, there are certain natural and rare traits and predispositions that set people on the proper track toward living philosophic lives.

Socrates offers, in the immediate sequel, a fuller description of philosophy by speaking in terms of metaphor. Many people view philosophy as a bizarre activity and with intense suspicion mainly because they do not grasp what it is, and Socrates says that he can explain its nature better and more clearly by using images. Some of the most famous and memorable images from this, or any, section of the *Republic* include: the ship of state (488a–489a), which describes the philosopher's proper relationship to the rest of political society; the echoing rocks (492b–c), which speaks to the powerful effects of public opinion on the human soul; and the divided line (509d–511d), providing a classification for the things that are, both in visible reality and in intelligible reality. The image of the sun is another important element of Socrates' description of philosophy and the philosopher. He likens the idea of the good itself to the sun, explaining that the good plays a similar role for thinking as the sun does in seeing material, visible reality. The idea of the good is, therefore, a precondition for knowing, providing "the truth to the things known and [giving] the power to the one who knows" (508e). Glaucon, who is speaking with Socrates at this point

16 In Plato's *Apology of Socrates*, we witness Socrates describing his own activity in Athens as that of a "gadfly." His habit has been to "set upon the city . . . as though upon a great and well-born horse who is rather sluggish because of his great size and needs to be awakened." This quote is cited from 30e of the *Apology of Socrates*: Plato and Aristophanes, *Four Texts on Socrates*, trans. Thomas G. West and Grace Starry West (Ithaca: Cornell University Press, 1998).

17 For a broad survey of this approach, consider Peter G. Northouse, *Leadership: Theory and Practice*, 8th ed. (Thousand Oaks, CA: SAGE Publications, 2019), 19–42; or Gary Yukl and William L. Gardner, III, *Leadership in Organizations*, 9th ed. (New York: Pearson, 2020), 192–222.

in the conversation, refers to the "overwhelming beauty" (509a) of which Socrates speaks – an indication that he has come closer throughout the night's conversation (and presumably because of the influence of Socrates) to seeing the charming nature of the philosophic life much more clearly.

Philosophy as leadership: the allegory of the cave

These vivid illustrations are, however, not the most famous to be found in Plato's *Republic*. In a dialogue that can claim to be well-known for so many things about philosophy and philosophers, perhaps the most famous part of the work is Socrates' allegory of the cave. At the opening of Book Seven, Socrates expresses that the cave is "an image of our nature in its education and want of education" (514a). Indeed, the cave is the most dominant image representing education in the *Republic*, a text that, if we are to credit the famous comment by the 18th-century philosopher Jean-Jacques Rousseau in his novel *Émile*, is "the most beautiful educational treatise ever written."[18] This particular story told by Socrates is the most enduring image of education that we have even in the present day.

Now, before interpreting the allegory of the cave in some detail, it makes sense to note a relatively uncontroversial point, one that is almost a truism in the study of leadership: there are strong connections, even mutual dependencies, between leadership and education. For instance, those who claim that individuals can develop their capacities as leaders mean that leadership is something that can be learned – it requires the right kind of education, in other words.[19] But more than this, the word itself is etymologically a synonym for leadership, and perhaps perfectly so. Our word education is rooted in two Latin words: first, the preposition *e* or *ex*, meaning "out of" or "out from"; and then, the verb *ducere* meaning "to lead" or "to guide." The Latin verb *educere* can mean either "to educate" or "to lead forth, to conduct out from." It is illuminating also to note that the Latin word for leader, which is *dux*, is the noun related to the verb *ducere*, and is, of course, the word from which the Italians have gotten their own word *duce*. It is probably much

---

18 Jean-Jacques Rousseau, *Émile, or on Education*, trans. Allan Bloom (New York: Basic Books, 1979), 40.

19 For a classic statement on finding the right kind of education for teaching future leaders, see James MacGregor Burns, *Leadership* (New York: Harper Perennial Political Classics, 2010), 444–62. Thomas Cronin makes a subtle point about this theme when he says: "My own belief is that students cannot usually be taught to be leaders. But students, and anyone else for that matter, can profitably be exposed to leadership, discussions of leadership skills and styles, and leadership strategies and theories. Individuals can learn in their own mind the strengths as well as limitations of leadership." Thomas E. Cronin, "Thinking and Learning about Leadership," *Presidential Studies Quarterly* 14, no. 1 (1984): 33.

more commonly known that there was a leader in the 20th century of a very dubious reputation by the name of Benito Mussolini, who referred to himself as *Il Duce*, the leader – and, again, this Italian designation comes from the same Latin word that also gives us the English word education.

Socrates explains the image about two-thirds the way through the dialogue of the *Republic*. The immediate purpose of his turning to describe the cave is to support his description of philosophy, the philosopher, and philosophic education.[20] Imagine, Socrates says, a cave where, at the bottom, people are bound in chains and spend their entire lives looking at the natural cave wall. The chains in the image are significant: Socrates refers to the cave explicitly as a prison and to those bound in chains as fellow prisoners. Above them up the cave is a constructed wall, over which some other people are holding up puppets and artifacts of all kinds, statues of men and other animals, the images of which are projected onto the wall as shadows by the light of a fire. These flickering shadows on the wall represent all that the people enchained have ever seen and have ever known. Socrates explains, though, that at some point somebody releases one of the human beings from his chains and compels him to turn around, leading him up a road, past the puppets and the fire, and eventually out of the cave, in order to see the things of the world in the clear light of the sun.

If we look more closely at the cave image, it is clear that one's mind tends to gravitate toward the experience of the student, if we can call him or her that. After all, we readers of the *Republic* are ourselves students of Plato and it is therefore only natural to reflect on the following questions: what is the experience of education and what does it genuinely require; how does it feel to undergo a liberal and liberating education; and how, then, do those women and men properly educated relate to the rest of society – to one's fellow prisoners? But we might also ask a different question: does Socrates' image tell us anything about the identity of the educator?

The first thing to note is that it seems clear that there is, in fact, somebody who fulfills the role of an educator. The prisoner does not find that his or her chains spontaneously become loose. In other words, the opening of Plato's *Republic*, Book Seven, is not really an image of auto-didacticism – although, one must admit that it would be interesting to ask how the first

---

20 Socrates' word for education is not *educatio*, of course, because Plato wrote in Greek and not Latin. The word is *paideia*, rendered education or culture, and it is related to the word for child, *pais*; *paideia* being that thing you do to bring up a child (*pais*) toward culture. That said, the word *educatio*, hence our word education, implies bringing up or rearing children as well. More importantly, the classical idea of education encompasses elements that are universal and apply equally to true education in different regimes, whether Greece, or Rome, or our own.

prisoner was released, or how the chains were established originally. In a famous passage of text, Socrates tells us more about the first interaction between teacher and student:

> Now consider . . . what their release and healing from bonds and folly would be like if something of this sort were by nature to happen to them. Take a man who is *released* and *suddenly compelled* to stand up, to turn his neck around, to talk and look up toward the light; and who, moreover, in doing all this is in pain and, because he is dazzled, is unable to make out those things whose shadows he saw before. What do you suppose he'd say if *someone were to tell him* that before he saw silly nothings, while now, because he is somewhat nearer to what *is* and more turned toward being, he sees more correctly; and, in particular, *showing him* each of the things that pass by, were to *compel* the man to answer his questions about what they are? Don't you suppose he'd be at a loss and believe that what was seen before is truer than what is now shown?
>
> (515c–d, emphasis added)

Note the language of this passage as a way of filling out something of the project of the educator: *releasing* those prisoners in chains; *compelling* them to turn around and see; *telling* or explaining to them what is going on; *showing* them what is really true as opposed to what is a mere image of the truth. Students require artful and effective guides to lead them through the process, in part because the journey can be so disorienting to them. There can be real pain and bedazzlement in coming to see that the things you held as truths were not true, strictly speaking, but had the character of opinion. Education often involves coming to grips with the fact that one's previously held understanding of the world was incorrect, or at least insufficient. But what if you enjoyed how you viewed the world prior to taking part in education, or found those false opinions to be comforting? What if those opinions were constitutive of your very identity and conception of your place in the cosmos? It would be a hard pill to swallow to have to come to grips with that reality.

This is why Socrates plays around with the imagery and language of compulsion in his allegory of the cave. In the sequel to the passage just quoted, Socrates says that "if . . . someone *dragged him away* from there *by force* along the rough, steep, upward way and didn't let him go before he had dragged him out into the light of the sun, wouldn't he be distressed and annoyed at being so dragged" (515e, emphasis added)? We see, then, this idea of force in dragging somebody up the cave, of compulsion or even coercion, as a symbol of just how dearly these people hold their most cherished opinions. It might take a little shaking to break them free. It is important for another reason as well: because Socrates intends to contrast this imagery of compulsion and coercion with his own vision of true education. In other words, force or coercion, as just described, is ultimately incompatible with the task of the educator.

Now, on one hand, most everyone would recognize that the life of reason operates according to the principle of necessary compulsion in an important way. Reasons or arguments are compelling in that they – provided they are valid reasons or arguments – should have the power to convince you of the truth of something. Reasons demonstrate to you how things are, necessarily, and in these cases, seeing with the mind's eye is truly believing. Indeed, the word that Socrates uses for "compel" throughout the cave image is the verb *anangkazo*, implying *anangkē*, or necessity. Still, and on the other hand, the educator simply cannot employ coercion in the process of education, as if one were to browbeat the student into seeing certain truths or to speak to him or her in a hectoring tone. The effect of such a practice would be either to induce dogmatic conviction or to turn the student off – or even worse, as we shall see.

We readers of Plato's *Republic* understand that this image of education as dragging others by force is not representative of Socrates' own views because, in the next speech, Socrates raises the possibility that the student traveling up the cave can become accustomed to what he or she sees. This makes the journey a little bit easier. The word here is *sunētheias*, meaning habituation or custom, and containing the word *ēthos*, the disposition or character of a human being – a word that will become particularly important for us in Chapter 3, on Aristotle's *Nicomachean Ethics*. Education, Socrates implies, can and should operate according to a strategy of accustomation, as it were – a strategy that satisfies two immediate aims. First, a student who properly becomes accustomed to this change in orientation both inside and outside the cave, and whose eyes are given the time to adjust to the light, will be more likely to see things clearly as they are, whether they are near the bottom of the cave close to the puppet masters, or emerging into the light of day. Whereas once there was a disorienting haze, now there is clarity. The second objective of this strategy relates more directly to the relationship between teacher and student. By managing education so that the student's eyes gradually come to see things as they are, the disposition of the student is affected, such that he or she is less likely to become distressed and annoyed both at the process of education itself and toward the teacher. It is hard not to recall here that the actual history of Socrates involves citizens of Athens who were distressed and annoyed at what Socrates was doing, to such an extent that they famously brought charges against this man and executed him.

We readers arrive, soon after these passages, at Socrates' succinct concept of education. Education is not the injection of knowledge or wisdom into empty souls, such that it represents a filling up of an empty vessel with knowledge, as in learning the facts that will make one a champion at trivia games. The educated woman or man will probably know a lot of those things, of course; but that is not education per se. Rather, because all souls have the power to see things more or less clearly, education involves turning the instrument with which one learns around from "that which is coming into being, together with the whole soul, until it is able to endure looking at that which is and the brightest part of that which is," which Socrates has referred to as "the good." There is an art, he says, of turning souls around in this way. That is the art that the educator practices (518c).

But, to conclude this close reading of Socrates' allegory, all of this means that true education demands the art of leadership, for the reasons enumerated to this point. In fact, true education *is* leadership – meaning, the process of somebody (say, a teacher) turning somebody else (say, a student) around and leading him or her out from the darkness and into the light, or out of the darkness of the student's own cave and into the light of day. When we speak of the concept of leadership – and here we refer to both scholarly voices and our own opinions common to human beings – we tend to mean something that does not and cannot operate using coercion. Tyrants force or coerce others to do the things they want, but leaders *lead* others, meaning they help followers to direct their thoughts, behavior, and energy to new ends, without resorting to the use of blunt coercion. This seems entirely consistent with Socrates' view that education by means of strength or blunt compulsion is both illegitimate and ineffective. In sum, education, according to Socrates, not only depends on good leadership, but it also turns out, on a basic level, to be equivalent to leadership.

One of the most important upshots of our treatment of Plato's *Republic* on philosophy, the philosopher, and leadership is that it helps us to understand more precisely how an education in philosophy – broadly understood as a liberal education, as we have argued in Chapter 1 – can be a strong foundation for mature leadership. A liberal education helps students to see things as they are by helping them learn about the diverse fields of human knowledge through the liberal arts disciplines. Consider, for example, the mission of colleges or universities devoted to the liberal arts. Students in these institutions take courses in classics or history, sociology or chemistry, literature or political science, and so forth, with the aim of seeing the true features of our world in their particularities and as reflected through the lenses of these disciplines of study. Students are expected to learn broadly, taking courses from all kinds of disciplines and on different topics – perhaps topics that they are not naturally fond of, or even particularly good at. In other words, a liberal education works to expand the student's intellectual horizons by helping him or her grasp the world *more than* before and *in more correct terms* than before. It provides students with a much wider scope on the world around all of us and a much larger and richer vocabulary for understanding and explaining the world.

This notion of acquiring a wider and richer vocabulary is highly relevant to the task of leadership. The scholar of political science Peter Augustine Lawler has argued this point very effectively. Addressing the debate on the condition of higher education in the United States today, and arguing that the case to be made for a so-called "higher competence" in the liberal arts is still quite strong, Lawler puts forward an argument about the purpose of reading real books, ones that are not, say, "technical manuals or sources of information." His argument is striking in its Socratic and Platonic overtones:

> There's a strong correlation between high-level success in life and the size of one's active vocabulary. This may seem implausible at first, but the more words a person really knows, *the more he knows about the real world around him.* To know what a word means is to really grasp the (always imperfect, of course) correspondence between the word and a part of reality. It is also to understand *the limitations of words*, when they are vaguely or wrongly used. With that kind of knowledge comes a good deal of discipline and self-control. For example, there's a clear distinction between those who use today's expert techno-babble (about "disruptive innovation" and the like) seriously and those who are able to deploy such jargon ironically. The latter have both a better grasp of what is really going on and the ability to use what they know to their own advantage. *Leaders, we notice, typically express themselves both precisely and ironically, and they are very adept at both description and deception.* And there are obvious connections, of course, between being deeply literate and being innovative and creative in most areas of life.[21]

What Lawler does here is to provide a variation on Socrates' theme in the cave image, updated to our own present context, to demonstrate how an education upward through the cave helps widen one's grasp of reality. Leaders are often confronted by the need to navigate difficult circumstances and to fulfill the difficult task of providing new direction for a group of people. To be able to draw on a rich vocabulary, to understand what it is to use irony

---

21 Peter Augustine Lawler, "Truly Higher Education," *National Affairs* 25 (Spring 2015): 127 (emphasis added).

and even deception when needed, and to be innovative and creative when
the conditions call for it – all of these tasks of leadership are supported
by a philosophic education, broadly understood. The knowledge one gains
through a liberal education, moreover, supports the virtues of discipline
and self-control in the student – virtues that are self-evidently important for
leadership.

Dion of Syracuse

In Chapter 5, we will take an extended look at the case study of Bill Gates,
founder of Microsoft Corporation. Far from being a flawless illustration
of the Platonic "philosopher king," Gates nevertheless serves as a recent
example of a leader whose enthusiastic attention to learning, both widely
and deeply, has had an impact on his leadership. Yet there is, in many ways,
a better case study for helping us understand the connection between Plato's
teaching in the *Republic* and leadership: Dion of Syracuse (408–354 BC),
who was a student and friend of Plato, in addition to being a crucial player
in the governance of his native city. The ancient biographer and moralist
Plutarch has expressed this thought near the beginning of his essay on the
life of Dion. Referring to both Dion and Marcus Junius Brutus, the famous
statesman of the late Roman Republic, Plutarch says that "they both bore
evidence to the truth of what their guide and teacher (i.e. Plato) said, that,
without the concurrence of power and success, with justice and prudence,
public actions do not attain their proper, great, and noble character."[22] This
is quite plainly a reference to Socrates' third proposed reform of the city in
the *Republic*, discussed earlier, in which philosophers are required to rule
the city as kings. For Plutarch, then, Dion's life helps us to see more clearly
Plato's thoughts on philosophy and leadership.[23]

Dion was the son of a prominent political family in Syracuse, a city
founded as a Greek outpost on Sicily and the principal political community on the island. He became the brother-in-law of the tyrant of Syracuse,

---

22 Plutarch, *Plutarch's Lives*, 537. We have taken all citations and translations of Plutarch
    in this chapter from the following edition: Plutarch, *Plutarch's Lives*, vol. 2, *The Dryden*,
    trans., ed. Arthur Hugh Clough (New York: The Modern Library, 2001).

23 Some readers may object to our reliance on Plutarch for the short case studies of Dion (in
    this chapter) and Alexander (in Chapter 3) because many scholars note that Plutarch is not
    particularly reliable as a historian. But we intend for these case studies to be thoughtful
    illustrations of the ideas in the philosophic texts of Plato and Aristotle, not perfect histo-
    ries. In the past, philosophers like Michel de Montaigne and Jean-Jacques Rousseau have
    sought human wisdom in the writings of Plutarch. For a contemporary source that takes
    Plutarch seriously as a thinker on political leadership, see Hugh Liebert, *Plutarch's Poli-
    tics: Between City and Empire* (New York: Cambridge University Press, 2016).

Dionysius I,[24] after the latter married Dion's sister Aristomache. But he was more than just family: celebrated for his intelligence, virtue, and spirit from an early age, Dion served Dionysius I as a trusted political advisor. Dion's connection with Plato was a serendipitous event for the young man, as Plato, traveling throughout Italy, made his way to Sicily and into the sphere of the court in Syracuse. Plutarch tells us about Dion's incredible intellectual talents. Despite his youth, "of all the scholars that attended Plato he was the quickest and aptest to learn, and the most prompt and eager to practice, the lessons of virtue. . . . [A]t the first taste of reason and a philosophy that demands obedience to virtue, his soul was set in a flame." Yet Dion also exhibited public spiritedness in his assumption about what philosophic learning should be for: "in the simple innocence of youth, concluding, from his own disposition, that the same reason would work the same effects upon Dionysius I, [Dion] made it his business, and at length obtained the favor of him . . . to hear Plato."[25] In other words, the young man expected Plato's lessons to be capable of improving the tyrant of Syracuse morally, thereby influencing him to rule the city more justly.

This expectation was not realized, however. Dionysius I took Plato to be criticizing him in his moral examinations and feared, ultimately, that the philosopher's ideas would destabilize his rule. Rooted in "the simple innocence of youth," as Plutarch had said, Dion's plan to bring philosophy to bear on real political leadership failed to consider that not all leaders would be amenable to philosophy. Dionysius I banished Plato from Syracuse and had him sold into slavery (Plato's freedom was later purchased by another philosopher), and continued his rule. Once the death of Dionysius I seemed imminent, Dion took steps to succeed to formal political power in Syracuse. But on hearing of this plan, the tyrant's son, Dionysius II, poisoned his father and subsequently took the throne before his father could express his will.

Beyond being the kind of human being who would murder his own father, Dionysius II was a vastly different kind of person than Dion in other ways too. Dionysius I, deeply fearful of usurpers when alive, had cloistered his son in the acropolis of Syracuse and kept him from an education. As

24 The institution of tyranny in ancient Greece was not perfectly similar to how we think of tyrannical governance today. Specifically, the term was slightly more morally ambiguous than how we tend to use it. According to A. Andrewes, a "tyrant was roughly what we should call a dictator, a man who obtained sole power in the state and held it in defiance of any constitution that had existed previously." That said, a tyrant "is not necessarily a wicked ruler, but he is an autocrat (and generally a usurper) who provides a strong executive." A. Andrewes, *The Greek Tyrants* (New York: Harper & Row, 1963), 7.
25 Plutarch, *Plutarch's Lives*, 539.

a consequence of this unfortunate upbringing, the governance of Dionysius II was a decadent one, replete with vulgar displays. His court was full
of flatters, scoundrels, and dissemblers – the perfect stereotype of a corrupt,
hedonistic political court. Even so – and, quite frankly, in an amazing turn
of events – Dion was successful in persuading the new tyrant to invite Plato
back to Syracuse. He believed that Plato could successfully teach Dionysius
II something about moral virtue, thereby persuading him to clean up his dic-
tatorship and lead Syracuse in accordance with the rule of law. Plutarch tells
us that Plato agreed to the plan, despite his troubles in Syracuse in recent
years, because he sought to demonstrate that his ideas about justice and
politics were not merely theoretical, but could also be applied to practice.[26]
And, in perhaps another amazing turn of events, the philosophic learning
administered by Plato seemed to have a positive influence on Dionysius II,
so much so that the tyrant said in public that he no longer wished to rule a
tyrannical regime.

This was, however, far too much for the members of the Syracusan court
to take. Led by the corrupt nobleman Philistus, a group of Dion's enemies
spoke ill of him to Dionysius II and persuaded the tyrant to banish Dion
from the city. Dionysius II confined Plato safely in the citadel of Syracuse
for a short time, eventually granting the philosopher his freedom to return
to Athens. But the pleasures of philosophic learning seem to have had an
enduring impact on the tyrant, because he continued to pursue them by
inviting many learned individuals into his court, debating them using Plato's arguments – "often incorrectly," as Plutarch clarifies. Frustrated by his
inability to advance in this kind of learning, Dionysius II invited Plato back
to Syracuse for a third time. And, in what is surely the most surprising twist
in this fascinating history, the philosopher accepted the invitation. Plato's
return to the court in Syracuse brought great "hopes to the Sicilians, who
were earnest in their prayers and good wishes that Plato might get the better
of Philistus, and philosophy triumph over tyranny."[27] Alas, these prayers
and wishes went unanswered, as Plato came to discover that he could have
no positive impact on Dionysius II and, therefore, on Syracuse. He returned
to Athens for the remainder of his life.

Another reason for Dionysius II to have invited Plato back to his court
was that he wanted to smooth over his rough relationship with Dion. In
his banishment from Syracuse, Dion traveled widely and spent much time
at Plato's Academy in Athens, deepening his study in philosophy, but ran
into trouble when the envious Dionysius II prevented him from accessing

---

26 Plutarch, *Plutarch's Lives*, 543.
27 Plutarch, *Plutarch's Lives*, 547–8.

money from his estates. Yet the courtship of Plato was not successful in this objective either, as Dion became only angrier with the tyrant for his exploitation of his teacher. Dion's return to his native city was through an organized attack on Syracuse, with the intention of toppling the tyranny, changing the regime, taking power, and ruling in accordance with law. He was successful in leading the rebellion and, once Dionysius II and his court were banished to the citadel, was elected to the governorship of Syracuse. Dion was finally in a position of public leadership where he could leverage real power for the good of his city.

Yet, promising as that may sound, the conclusion of the history of Dion is not a happy one. Despite having been triumphant in overthrowing the tyranny, Dion discovered that he was not especially skilled in engaging with the people of Syracuse. One problem was "the dislike they had taken to Dion's grave and stately manner, which they thought overbearing and assuming."[28] Doubtless this disposition was rooted in Dion's nature, but it is not unreasonable to assume that his education in Platonic philosophy amplified it, considering Plato's heavy emphasis on virtue and the rarity of true philosophy. Dion also had learned from Plato the benefits of overcoming the passions of anger and envy – even if those passions arise in response to his mortal political enemies – not to mention the idea that pity is preferable to vengeance. Yet, while philosophically sound, these notions may be politically inexpedient: Plutarch clarifies that the laws, by contrast, "determine it juster to revenge an injury than to do an injury."[29] Another problem was that the people had just been liberated from their subjection to a tyranny, yet Dion would not gratify them by instituting democratic reforms. Like "a good physician," he "endeavored to keep the city to a strict and temperate regimen."[30] Dion came into conflict with a faction led by Heracleides, who was much more willing to modify the regime of Syracuse in line with democratic principles. For example, he pushed for a redistribution of lands among all citizens equally. Dion struggled with the political forces internal to his city for the rest of his days, never once establishing a stable political community for his native city, and was finally assassinated in a coup orchestrated by Dionysius II.

What, then, and to conclude, is the essential insight we should take from this brief history of Dion, Plato, and Syracuse? Despite Plato's teaching on true philosophy as providing the essential underpinning of sound leadership, it would be a good idea to proceed with a healthy dose of caution when applying that teaching to actual leadership in and for the public. Dion

---

28 Plutarch, *Plutarch's Lives*, 557.
29 Plutarch, *Plutarch's Lives*, 566.
30 Plutarch, *Plutarch's Lives*, 560.

seems, in some respects, to be an exemplar of all that is best in humanity: he passionately devoted himself to the cause of philosophy and virtue, as well as to doing good for his native city, throughout his entire life. But this singular focus on using Platonic philosophy to inform his leadership – not to mention the leadership of both tyrants, father and son – failed to consider the significant gap between the principles of Platonic education and the whole regime of Syracuse. Perhaps, if Dion had reflected on the points of dissonance between philosophy and the political regime, he may have discovered more effective ways of instituting positive reforms for Syracuse, changes that were not perfectly good but workable all the same. Or, perhaps he would have done as his teacher Plato did, deciding to turn away from political leadership and toward education – which is, as we have outlined in our discussion of Plato's *Republic*, a very real kind of leadership itself. We recall something noted earlier in this chapter, that the city in speech of the *Republic* was intended not as a blueprint for the reform of political leadership in the real world, but rather as a heuristic device for comprehending the true nature of philosophy more completely.

Of course, we leave it to readers to determine the most important lessons from the case of Dion, and by that same token to conclude how Bill Gates, in Chapter 5, may illuminate Plato's ideas on leadership and the philosopher, that most virtuous of human beings. Our next task, however, is to turn to Plato's student Aristotle and his examination of a different kind of virtue, moral virtue, and its significance for the character of our leaders.

Bibliography

Andrewes, A. *The Greek Tyrants*. New York: Harper & Row, 1963.

Bauman, David C. "Plato on Virtuous Leadership: An Ancient Model for Modern Business." *Business Ethics Quarterly* 28, no. 3 (2018): 251–74.

Bloom, Allan. *The Republic of Plato*. 2nd ed. Translated with Notes and an Interpretive Essay. New York: Basic Books, 1968.

Burns, James MacGregor. *Leadership*. New York: Harper Perennial Political Classics, 2010.

Ciulla, Joanne B. "Plato (c. 428-c. 348 BCE)." In *Encyclopedia of Leadership*, edited by George R. Goethels, Georgia J. Sorenson, and James MacGregor Burns, 1202–6. Thousand Oaks, CA: Sage Publications, 2004.

Cooper, Laurence D. "Beyond the Tripartite Soul: The Dynamic Psychology of the *Republic*." *Review of Politics* 63, no. 2 (2001): 341–72.

Cronin, Thomas E. "Thinking and Learning about Leadership." *Presidential Studies Quarterly* 14, no. 1 (1984): 22–34.

Cronin, Thomas E., and Michael A. Genovese. *Leadership Matters: Unleashing the Power of Paradox*. Boulder: Paradigm Publishers, 2012.

Finkelberg, Margalit. *The Gatekeeper: Narrative Voice in Plato's Dialogues*. Leiden, NLD: Brill, 2019.

Flanigan, Jessica. "Philosophical Methodology and Leadership Ethics." *Leadership* 14, no. 6 (2018): 707–30.

Forde, Steven. "Gender and Justice in Plato." *American Political Science Review* 91, no. 3 (1997): 657–70.

Kalligas, Paul, Chloe Balla, Effie Baziotopoulou-Valavani, and Vassilis Karasmanis, eds. *Plato's Academy: Its Workings and Its History*. Cambridge: Cambridge University Press, 2020.

Lawler, Peter Augustine. "Truly Higher Education." *National Affairs* 25 (Spring 2015): 114–30.

Liebert, Hugh. *Plutarch's Politics: Between City and Empire*. New York: Cambridge University Press, 2016.

Nendza, James. "Nature and Convention in Book V of the *Republic*." *Canadian Journal of Political Science* 21, no. 2 (1988): 331–57.

Nietzsche, Friedrich. *Beyond Good and Evil: Prelude to a Philosophy of the Future*. Translated by Walter Kaufmann. New York: Vintage Books, 1989.

Northouse, Peter G. *Leadership: Theory and Practice*. 8th ed. Thousand Oaks, CA: Sage Publications, 2019.

Plato. *Epistles*. Translated by Glenn Morrow. Indianapolis: Bobbs-Merrill, 1962.

———. *Symposium*. Translated by Seth Benardete. Chicago: University of Chicago Press, 2001.

Plato, and Aristophanes. *Four Texts on Socrates*. Rev. ed. Translated with Notes by Thomas G. West and Grace Starry West. Ithaca, NY: Cornell University Press, 1989.

Plutarch. *Plutarch's Lives*. Vol. 2 of the Dryden Translation. Edited with Preface by Arthur Hugh Clough. New York: The Modern Library, 2001.

Powell, Jonathan, and Niall Rudd. "Introduction." In Cicero, *The Republic and The Laws*, translated by Niall Rudd, with an Introduction and Notes by Jonathan Powell and Niall Rudd, ix–xxxi. Oxford: Oxford University Press, 1998.

Price, Terry L. *Leadership Ethics: An Introduction*. New York: Cambridge University Press, 2008.

Rousseau, Jean-Jacques. *Émile, or on Education*. Translated with an Introduction and Notes by Allan Bloom. New York: Basic Books, 1979.

Saxonhouse, Arlene W. "The Philosopher and the Female in the Political Thought of Plato." *Political Theory* 4, no. 2 (1976): 195–212.

Strauss, Leo. *Natural Right and History*. Chicago: University of Chicago Press, 1965.

Takala, T. "Plato on Leadership." *Journal of Business Ethics* 17 (1998): 785–98.

Wren, J. Thomas, ed. *The Leader's Companion: Insights on Leadership through the Ages*. New York: The Free Press, 1995.

Yukl, Gary, and William L. Gardner, III. *Leadership in Organizations*. 9th ed. New York: Pearson, 2020.

3   Aristotle

Character ethics, greatness of soul, and leadership

In the first three chapters of this book, we trace a chain of influence beginning with Socrates, the one responsible for bringing philosophy down from the heavens – in Cicero's colorful description – and directing it to be concerned with humanity. And if our analysis of Plato's *Republic* is on the mark, then this influence in the form of philosophic education should be seen as a kind of leadership, one that can provide a model for us. Plato was the greatest student of Socrates and spread his influence to his own students. Plato's own greatest student was Aristotle (384–322 BC), who studied for about 20 years with his teacher at the Academy before directing his own school in Athens at the Lyceum, named for the temple dedicated to Apollo Lyceus at which the school was located, close to the Athenian Acropolis.

Like his teacher, Aristotle appears to have had some connection with actual political leadership – a fact that remains one of the more famous notes in the pages of this most famous philosopher's biography. General tradition tells us that Aristotle was the tutor of a young Alexander after having been invited to Macedon, a kingdom in the northeastern part of the Greek peninsula, for that role by Alexander's father, Philip. We will close this current chapter by returning to the question of Aristotle's education of Alexander and the influence it may have had on the student's leadership qualities. But, for now, we want to notice something plainly obvious that provides a helpful access point into our discussion of Aristotle's ideas. Everyone who understands something about Alexander – and, frankly, even most people who do not know much about him – know that he is commonly described as "The Great." To speak of somebody in these specific terms, however, is to highlight the notion of personal character, or at least to raise the question of character. What was it about Alexander that made him so *great*? What aspects of his soul – in other words, those personal qualities that go beyond external, material goods, or the scope of one's worldly influence – made for his greatness?

There is arguably no better guide for a serious discussion of character than Aristotle, who provided a deep and rich treatment of these questions in his *Nicomachean Ethics*. Named after either Aristotle's father or son, both of whom were called Nicomachus, the text dates to the fourth century BC. The *Nicomachean Ethics* is composed of ten Books that explore a multitude of topics, such as happiness as the end of human pursuits, habituation and character, moral and intellectual virtues, and friendship. More important to our purpose is that it has many clear, even obvious, connections to the study of leadership. Aristotle wrote this text, in part, to explore the moral experience of a particular class of men in the Greek city who held positions of public leadership. That Aristotle's philosophic commentary on character also, and at the same time, bears on matters that are universally true to humankind as a whole is proof of this philosopher's own greatness. The *Nicomachean Ethics* has been an essential source for informing both the education and self-understanding of leaders throughout the ages. One illuminating story concerns Winston Churchill, Prime Minister of England during World War II and one of the most remarkable political leaders of the 20th century. In the 1920s, Churchill was given a copy of Aristotle's text by his friend Lord Birkenhead, who told him that some thought this was the greatest book ever written. Churchill returned it several weeks later saying (in effect) that it was quite interesting, but that he had already thought it all out for himself. In other words, Churchill took his magnanimous perspective on moral questions to be identical to Aristotle's. The *Ethics* was a mirror of his soul.[1]

Our aim in this chapter is to provide an accessible discussion of Aristotle's *Nicomachean Ethics*, drawing out essential lessons for leadership one can discover in this text. We begin with a brief look at the structure of the book and then move to explain the core elements of Aristotle's moral theory, including his emphasis on happiness, the concept of character and how one comes to develop it, and the meaning of virtue. Unlike in the previous chapter, which presented a close reading of the majority of Plato's *Republic*, we have chosen here to focus our presentation on one of Aristotle's moral virtues in particular: *megalopsychia*, or greatness of soul. Not only is this virtue profoundly important to Aristotle's ethical philosophy – after all, he refers to greatness of soul as one of the "peaks" of virtue (along with justice,

---

1 The political theorist Robert Faulkner would appear to agree with this assessment: "Among the seminal ancient accounts of human excellence . . . only [Aristotle's, *Nicomachean Ethics*] adequately illuminates the mixture of greatness and goodness to be found in, say, Washington or Winston Churchill." Robert K. Faulkner, *The Case for Greatness: Honorable Ambition and Its Critics* (New Haven, CT: Yale University Press, 2007), 18.

which is the other) – but also proper reflection on this virtue promises to illuminate questions of leadership uniquely. This is partly because the ideal of greatness of soul seems to be rather contrary to our own sensibilities as citizens of liberal democracies, who practice models of leadership that are consistent with liberal democracy. Aristotle's philosophy, then, may offer us a contrasting view of good leadership – but a view that is not ultimately as remote or unapproachable as it originally appears.

Happiness, habituation, and character

Unlike Plato's *Republic*, which is a dialogue presenting a conversation among several characters, none of whom are Plato, Aristotle's *Nicomachean Ethics* is a treatise. Simply put, this written form sets out to give a treatment of a particular theme in the author's own voice. In the case of this text, the theme is ethics (*ethika*), by which Aristotle means one's character. The complete text is divided into ten Books, which are themselves divided into Chapters – although scholars are fairly certain that these divisions did not originate with Aristotle, but rather were made by a later editor. After first raising the question of the proper end of the human being and explaining the concept of character in Books One and Two, Aristotle covers moral choice and enumerates 11 moral virtues in Books Three through Five. The remainder of the text investigates a broad array of themes, such as intellectual virtue, self-restraint, friendship, and the central role of contemplation in a well-ordered life.

In one of the most famous opening lines in the history of philosophy, Aristotle begins the *Nicomachean Ethics* by laying out the wide parameters for his study. "Every art and every inquiry, and similarly every action as well as choice, is held to aim at some good" (1094a).[2] In other words, everything that occurs in our human experience points toward some end, meaning that it has some purpose; nothing is idle in the sense that it happens just randomly, with no direction. Individual human beings do everything they do, in both action and thought, precisely because they believe that it is good for them to do it. The question then becomes: what is this good that serves to orient humanity? In Book One, Chapter Five, Aristotle lists a number of possible answers, including pleasure, honor, contemplation, and money – all of which miss the mark for various reasons. The ultimate good, which is that thing for

---

2 All citations to Aristotle's *Nicomachean Ethics* will be made in parentheses according to the margin numbers that are standard in all editions of the text. For translations of the *Nicomachean Ethics*, we have used the following edition: Aristotle, *Aristotle's Nicomachean Ethics*, trans., with an interpretive essay, notes, and glossary, Robert C. Bartlett and Susan D. Collins (Chicago: University of Chicago Press, 2011).

the sake of which people do anything, would have to be not only *the best*, meaning complete or perfect, something humans would choose for itself and not for the sake of something else, but also *self-sufficient*, meaning "that which makes life choiceworthy and in need of nothing" (1097b15). Aristotle says that this good is happiness. It is what we would choose with an end to nothing more. Humans might want certain things like money or friends, children or a good reputation, because we think they would make us happy, but we do not want happiness because we think we can get anything more out of it: it is at "the end" of our experience as humans. Happiness is, for Aristotle, the condition of human flourishing.[3]

But if happiness is indeed the ultimate good for human beings, then what is the proper work of humanity so that we may live and flourish in line with this good? Aristotle says that human beings are distinguished from other natural beings by their possession of reason (*logos*), or their ability to think and to converse with one another about the most important subjects, and that a proper human life is an active life. If, he continues,

> we posit the work of a human being as a certain life, and this is an activity of soul and actions accompanied by reason, the work of a serious man being to do these things well and nobly, and each thing is brought to completion well in accord with the virtue proper to it – if this is so, then *the human good becomes an activity of soul in accord with virtue, and if there are several virtues, then in accord with the best and most complete one.*
>
> [1098a13–19; emphasis added]

Aristotle's point here is that human nature admits of certain virtues – or in other words "excellences," the attainment of which permits the human being to do its work or activity well. The truly good life consists in the operation of these virtues in their peak condition. Contrary to the more modern relativistic argument saying that no manner of living is truly better or worthy of being more privileged than any other, Aristotle holds that nature prescribes the right way to live for human beings. If this is true, then the life in accordance with virtue is the happy life.

What, ultimately, is "the life in accordance with virtue"? What does it look like, and how does one come to it? Aristotle argues in the *Nicomachean Ethics* that human beings are not born – and we do not live as

---

3 Robert Bartlett and Susan Collins refer to this book simply as "a treatise on happiness." Robert Bartlett and Susan Collins, "Introduction," in Aristotle, *Aristotle's Nicomachean Ethics*, trans., with an interpretive essay, notes, and glossary, Robert C. Bartlett and Susan D. Collins (Chicago: University of Chicago Press, 2011), xiii.

children – with the virtues, even though we are born with the capacity for virtue. Rather, the development of our mature moral capacities requires a long and comprehensive education, which begins at an early age. Human beings become morally virtuous most importantly through action and the correct kind of repeated activity. And it makes all the difference what kind of activities are pursued. For instance, in order to become courageous, Aristotle explains that one must do things "in terrifying circumstances by being habituated to feel fear or confidence" (1103b16–17). The activity must be done properly and in the right manner, and Aristotle indicates that virtue tends to arise in those things that are most difficult (1105a10). In general, the process according to which the human being develops the virtues, and his or her soul becomes etched deeply with these qualities, is habituation in the correct activities. The Greek word for habit is *ethos*, which is the source of our word "ethics." At a young age, a person begins to practice certain ways of living and acting in the world that develop into securely held habits, functioning as almost a second nature.

The activities done in line with the virtues are correct, for Aristotle, if and only if the moral agent is in a specific condition: "first, if he acts knowingly; second, if he acts by choosing and by choosing the actions in question for their own sake; and third, if he acts while being in a steady and unwavering state" (1105a31–33). Yet it seems as if the first of these conditions is the least important, for Aristotle goes on to say that "when it comes to the virtues, knowledge has no or little force" (1105b3). In other words, when a human being has undergone the process of habituation correctly, his or her moral activity does not rely on the ability to reason about it authoritatively during the moment of actively practicing the virtue. It is, rather, a condition of soul that is something like the phenomenon of muscle memory in a physical body.

Through this upbringing, undertaken in the correct way, a human being will have developed a characteristic (*hexis*) of soul that is the basis of a mature moral virtue. Note, importantly, that a virtue is not equivalent to a habit. Habit is where the educational process begins, but there is an element of choice involved, and one cannot be virtuous if one does something accidentally: it has to be done in a steady and unwavering state. As Arthur Melzer, scholar of Aristotle's political philosophy, explains,

> Perhaps the best, if imperfect English term for [*hexis*] would be a *disposition*, a settled disposition, although one might speak also of an "attitude." This seems correct. If we consider our inner lives, we have not only particular momentary desires strung together like beads on a string, but also settled, organized ways of desiring and reacting that extend over time, that are relatively fixed, that involve choice or

decision, and that knit together our appetitive life into a pattern and a whole. We have settled dispositions and attitudes. A disposition in this sense is not a desire, but rather a stance or posture toward desires – an attitude. And it is rooted in reflection and choice: it is a settled way of looking at, evaluating, and treating our own desires.[4]

This phenomenon, again, is what Aristotle means when he speaks of a person's character – and, to a very large extent, this is precisely what we mean as well.

Virtue and our (half-hearted) critique of honor in the modern world

One simple way of making sense of the Aristotelian concept of virtue is to ask the question, "how should one characterize a good person?" If virtue is a specific excellence that makes a person good – or, in other words, that allows the human being to do his or her activity as well as possible – then what are those qualities? From the middle of Book Two through Book Five of the *Nicomachean Ethics*, Aristotle outlines an answer to these questions, focusing on the experience of moral virtue.[5] Aristotle provides a treatment of 11 moral virtues in total, along with their corresponding vices. Virtue, he says, resides

> in the mean relative to us . . ., a mean with respect to two vices, the once vice related to excess, the other to deficiency; and further, it is a mean because some vices fall short of and others exceed what should be the case in both passions and actions, whereas virtue discovers and chooses the middle term.
>
> (1106b36–1107a6)

The particular moral virtues that Aristotle explores in this text are: courage, moderation, liberality, magnificence, greatness of soul, ambition, gentleness, friendliness, truthfulness, wittiness, and justice.

Exercising these virtues depends on having the appropriate feeling and performing the proper action in a particular context. For example, one

---

4 Arthur M. Melzer, "Character vs. Free Will: Aristotle and Kant on Moral Responsibility," in *In Search of Humanity. Essays in Honor of Clifford Orwin*, ed. Andrea Radasanu (Lanham, MD: Lexington Books, 2015), 438–9 (emphasis in original).
5 Later in the text, Aristotle explores the intellectual virtues – concepts that roughly correspond to what Plato is driving at in the *Republic* with his discussion of philosophy. Because of the extended treatment of those themes in Chapter 2, we will focus on the theme of moral virtue in Aristotle's thinking here in the present chapter.

becomes courageous by forming the right disposition to fear. When confronted by the fearful thing, too much courage leads to rashness, while too little is the mark of cowardice. Courage is the mean between these extremes. The mean is not a recipe of equal parts rashness and timidity; instead, it is the situational know-how and ability to face fear in a way that is just right. For Aristotle, the height of courage is self-sacrifice in defense of something more significant than the individual. War tests a soldier's mettle and is the proper arena for the virtue of courage to be on full display (1115b3–5).

As the bedrock of the Greek *polis*, or city, courage is born from political necessity. Robust citizen-soldiers made all the difference in a world in which communities lived under a perpetual threat. Due to its significance, Aristotle examines courage first, but he does not uncritically accept this heroic virtue. He observes that courage can be harmful to the individual since death in battle, as noble as that might be, robs this person of the chance to continue the quest to happiness by living virtuously.

The other virtues demand less. Moderation seeks to temper one's desires for food, drink, and sex. Liberality decries stinginess and profligacy and helps a virtuous person properly spend his money. There is also magnificence, which involves large expenditures. Magnificence avoids the extremes of cheapness or tackiness, on one hand, and contemptible ostentation, on the other. But just having one or two of these virtues is not sufficient for someone to live the full moral life that Aristotle has in mind in the *Ethics*. He reserves greatness of soul as that characteristic that gives complete meaning to a life devoted to virtue ethics.

Aristotle's Greek word *megalopsychia* literally means "greatness of soul" – the standard translation of the word in English is magnanimity or proper pride. The Latinized "magnanimity" is a loan-translation from the Greek. There are, however, critical differences between Aristotle's notion of greatness of soul and the contemporary meaning of magnanimity. Today, the word means high-mindedness, which is something characterized by generosity and kindness. A magnanimous leader, for example, is gracious with political opponents. Winston Churchill's maxim comes to mind, "In Victory, Magnanimity." Although Aristotle's great-souled man must be generous, the philosopher describes this person as an ethical paragon of aristocratic virtue. In fact, the great-souled man is one of two pinnacles of moral excellence, which is something that makes him deserving of the highest honors.[6] This man is a rare type and seems to hold an exalted place in Aristotle's examination of the virtues.

---

6 Among the ethical virtues in the first five books of the *Ethics,* there are two peaks: greatness of soul (IV.3) and universal justice (V.1).

For the sake of rendering Aristotle's intended meaning as clear as possible, while remaining consistent with the translation of the *Ethics* we have chosen, we opt for "greatness of soul" (*megalopsychia*) and "great-souled man" (*megalopsychos*).[7] Greatness of soul is not only distinct from the other virtues in the *Ethics*, but also a considerable departure from present expectations for leadership, morality, and gender equality. Rather than skirt criticism, we give voice to the idea that greatness of soul is downright questionable. There may be incompatibilities worth noticing between modern beliefs and norms, and this ancient virtue. Because Christianity and liberal democracy have shaped the West and pushed the Greeks aside, in this critique we emphasize the notions of self-satisfied pride and honor-seeking. Second, after pulling down greatness of soul from its pedestal, we then try to raise it out from the rubble. We relax our skeptical approach, identifying the resemblances and sympathies that still exist between modern perceptions of greatness and Aristotle's idea.

We begin by taking stock of the foremost reasons why a modern Western audience ought to remain on their guard about this ancient virtue. For the sake of brevity, we identify this person as the reader. In his discussion of the great-souled man, Aristotle never mentions the common lot of men, women, children, and slaves. Do these groups not have moral souls, too? Even the name itself, the great-souled man, smacks of blindness. To add to our estrangement from this idea is the great-souled man's narrow preoccupation with his greatness and honors. Aristotle seems to be lionizing the megalomaniacal ambitions of the few who, in antiquity, sought the splendid honor of kingly rule and divine comparison.[8] Did not his premier student, Alexander the Great, try to command from these hubristic heights?

To consider the idea of honor is to stumble up an ancient ruin. In our progressive era, the reader chafes at honor's connotations of physical strength, political mastery and control, and perverse masculinities. Honor is, however, a crucial component of the great-souled man's sense of worth. If honor is a non-starter for our reader, then the great-souled man is dead upon arrival. Honor is an anachronism. One can imagine a classic western cowboy walking into a hipster bar in Greenwich Village, New York City. No one cares that he is the quickest draw and that he is ready to defend this

---

7 Although we could use the ungendered translation, "great-souled one," it is clear that Aristotle is working with conventional gendered roles in the *Ethics*. If we adopt Aristotle's usage, then the reader shall be in the place to cast her ultimate judgment whether Aristotle's philosophy is open to the suggestion of a great-souled woman and non-elites, or whether we must necessarily amend his thought for the sake of being inclusive.

8 Roger Brock, *Greek Political Imagery from Homer to Aristotle* (London: Bloomsbury Publishing, 2013), esp. 1–24.

honor against any man. Likewise, can one fathom the idea of calling upon one's second and drawing pistols at 20 paces? Despite the distance between honor and contemporary society, we ought to cover our basis by asking, "what happened to honor?"

In the United States, for example, a dominant post-honor society began to take shape after the Vietnam War.[9] Broadly speaking, the word itself has come to mean a Victorian and prudish concern for women's virtue.[10] Where honor cultures still exist, psychologists find higher incidences of poor mental health, destructive social behavior, and violence.[11] For anthropologists, honor cultures are a symbol of a "primitive mind."[12] Psychologists conceive that honor is a fetishized virtue that produces self-sustaining social conditions and economies of injustice, and where honor is absent, they observe peace among human beings.[13]

Democratic societies deem honor-seeking as incompatible with the values of equality, dignity, and fairness.[14] Enlightenment thinkers, primarily Thomas Hobbes, downgraded honor, arguing that it was crude and irrational. Consequently, Hobbes labored in his book *Leviathan* to demonstrate that an individual's self-interest always trumped honor. Later, John Locke adopted Hobbes's argument in favor of individual self-interest, but he reversed Hobbes's justification for absolutism into a defense of liberal democracy.[15]

The Judeo-Christian tradition strikes at the core of an honor culture by raising humility to the highest virtue, while the essential vice – the utmost evil – is pride.[16] Moreover, guilt takes the place of shame, which is the corollary of honor. Humility finds widespread approval in secular ethics

9 James Bowman, *Honor: A History* (New York: Encounter Books, 2007), 235.
10 See Katherine U. Henderson and Barbara F. McManus, *Half Humankind: Contexts and Texts of the Controversy about Women in England, 1540–1640* (Champaign: University of Illinois Press, 1985).
11 See Ryan P. Brown, *Honor Bound: How a Cultural Ideal Has Shaped the American Psyche* (New York: Oxford University Press, 2016); and Mark Conney, *Honor Cultures and Violence* (New York: Oxford University Press, 2013).
12 John Alan Cohan, *The Primitive Mind and Modern Man* (Sharjah, UAE: Bentham Science Publishers, 2010).
13 Steven Pinker, *The Better Angels of Our Nature: Why Violence Has Declined* (New York: Penguin Group, 2012).
14 For a classic discussion of honor in the United States and in democratic societies more generally, see Alexis de Tocqueville, *Democracy in America*, trans., ed., and with an intro. by Harvey C. Mansfield and Delba Winthrop (Chicago: University of Chicago Press, 2000), 589–99.
15 See Laurie M. Johnson, *Honor in America?: Tocqueville on American Enlightenment* (Lanham, MD: Lexington Books, 2016).
16 C.S. Lewis, *Mere Christianity* (New York: Simon and Schuster, 1996), 109.

as well, as it is the cornerstone of theories of servant leadership, cosmo-
politanism, and authenticity.[17] By contrast, scholars who try to rehabilitate
honor for a contemporary world engage in tortured apologetics.[18] From
the perspective of modern ethics, Aristotle's idea of a great-souled man
appears to be off the table. It fosters competition and comparison with others and a dangerous illusion of unfailing judgment and self-sufficiency.[19]
Further, there is no appetite for the recrudescence of a great man theory,
in which some members of society actively seek honor and glory as its
highest prize.

Honor is dead and self-satisfied pride is off-putting. But Aristotle's great-
souled man is complicated, and it could prove fruitful for the reader to take
their critical lenses off and put on their everyday and ordinary caps. Greatness of soul, it seems, still retains something of its luster in the ordinary
desire to see greatness embodied in people and things. We walk the readers
through some examples where such a desire not only is strong but also
shares in common with Aristotle's notion. In music and the arts, the practice of stacking up the greatest virtuosos points to a genuine admiration of
beautiful works that inspire wonder – aesthetic value, as we will discuss in
the following, matters a great deal in Aristotle's composition of the perfect
gentleman. There is also a maniacal obsession and endless opining about a
single sport's most celebrated and greatest athlete of all time, the G.O.A.T.
Although the end goal of athletic competition is itself not too important, the
discussion surrounding the G.O.A.T. requires a consideration of the qualities human beings possess beyond talent and practice, such as determina-
tion, poise, love of the game, and elevating one's teammates, to name a few.

Even Aristotle has something to say on the topic of athletics. In his work
Rhetoric, he observes that one of these qualities is the beauty of the balanced and harmonious body, especially that of pentathletes. What is beautiful in an athlete's body is conducive to athletic virtue: "bodily excellence in
athletics consists in size, strength, and swiftness of foot; for to be swift is to
be strong (1361b13)."[20] There is a connection between the good and beautiful condition of the body, on one hand, and the soul, on the other. Following

17 See Luis Cabrera, *The Humble Cosmopolitan: Rights, Diversity, and Trans-State Democ-
    racy* (New York: Oxford University Press, 2019); and Milton Sousa and Dirk van
    Dierendonck, "Servant Leadership and the Effect of the Interaction between Humility,
    Action, and Hierarchical Power on Follower Engagement," *Journal of Business Ethics*
    141, no. 1 (2017): 13–25.

18 See Tamler Sommers, *Why Honor Matters* (New York: Basic Books, 2018).

19 See Shawn R. Tucker, *Pride and Humility: A New Interdisciplinary Analysis* (New York:
    Palgrave Macmillan, 2016).

20 Aristotle, *The Rhetoric and the Poetics of Aristotle*, trans. W. Rhys Roberts and Ingram
    Bywater (New York: Modern Library, 1984).

this image of the athlete's virtue, we may say that the great-souled man is a moral athlete, and in regard to the field of virtue, he is the G.O.A.T.

The greatness theme also makes good entertainment. The movie industry has turned the comic book superhero into modern global mythology. Despite the character flaws of the heroes and constant quarreling among themselves, only these god-like characters seem able to tackle the problems of our world. Our only job is to sit back and munch on popcorn. There is, however, more to these movies than climactic battles and witty bantering between characters.[21]

The superhero most resembling an Aristotelian great-souled man is Marvel's T'Challa, a.k.a. Black Panther. A prince reared as an aristocrat, he suddenly becomes the warrior-king of his technologically advanced yet traditional society, Wakanda. He is also attended by an all-women and fiercely courageous royal guard. Not only is his courage tested, but also his prudence and justice, which proves unfailing. T'Challa loses his kingdom to a tyrannical ideologue, and he must navigate the murky waters of civil conflict, diplomacy, and global ethics. Although the film's plot is framed as a coming-of-age narrative, T'Challa is uniquely graceful and has a refinement of character unlike any other superhero. He never stoops or commits injustice; his sterling virtues are in perfect alignment with his unerring judgment.

One arena where a T'Challa would be most welcome but is sorely lacking is in America's politics, especially at the presidential level. There is an abiding expectation that a president will act "presidential." These native hopes are felt to the highest in the crucible of a national crisis when countries are facing war, domestic turmoil, natural disasters, and, for the foreseeable future, pandemics. It is in such circumstances that a public demands the rare combination of enduring character traits that unite the country, steers it clear from peril, and morally elevates the country's citizens. But such leaders are the exception. In discussions about American politics and history, the argument runs that great presidents are rare, George Washington and Abraham Lincoln rest head and shoulders above everyone else, and that there has been a long drought since the last great president, Franklin Delano Roosevelt.[22]

Why does the American public crave greatness in popular forms and in leadership? Why does it continue to heap admiration on these lionized

---

21 For a discussion of what the extreme popularity of superhero movies in our society reveals about ourselves, see Paul A. Cantor, *Pop Culture and the Dark Side of the American Dream: Con Men, Gangsters, Drug Lords, and Zombies* (Lexington: University of Kentucky Press, 2019), esp. 88–132.

22 See Marc Landy and Sidney M. Milkis, *Presidential Greatness* (Lawrence: University Press of Kansas, 2000).

figures and invent mythical ones onscreen? Despite the decline in the use of terms like character, virtue, and conscience, it is these enduring traits that people believe make all the difference in how one's life can meaningfully affect the lives of others.[23] Although the public imagination is captivated by greatness, today's discourse seems to lack the means to articulate its admiration for the moral goodness of one person who deserves such praise.

Even as modern society puts distance between itself and ancient forms, it becomes susceptible to a buried atavism. David Brooks, an op-ed columnist for the *New York Times*, wrote a book titled *The Road to Character*. It was a *New York Times* bestseller, and Brooks explicitly uses Aristotle's idea of greatness of soul to help explain the life and work of George Marshall.[24] Could such exceptions prove the rule?

In a smaller corner of the world, several scholars argue that historical leaders such as Pericles, George Washington, and Edmund Barton display civic-minded virtues and have a deeper understanding of themselves as reflected in Aristotle's great-souled man.[25] Even cases where an author does not model their ideas on Aristotle, they seem to gravitate to the notion of a great soul to describe figures as diverse as Nelson Mandela, Pope John Paul II, and Mother Theresa, among others.[26] Mohandas Gandhi, who was called Mahatma, "the great soul," is shown to be a complex study of political, intellectual, and spiritual character formation.[27] Although pyscho-biographical accounts are all the rage, a Freudian study of these former individuals' unconscious complexities, anxieties, and insecurities would not seem to do such persons justice.

Extraordinary leaders are human. They must suffer through their defects, fears, and pains. Abraham Lincoln battled melancholy, as did Winston Churchill, who called it his "black dog." If they were alive today, then they would likely be treated for clinical depression.[28] Yet it is the humanity of

---

23 See James Merritt, *Character Still Counts: It Is Time to Restore Our Lasting Values* (Eugene, OR: Harvest House Publishers, 2020).

24 See David Brooks, *The Road to Character* (New York: Random House, 2015), 127–8.

25 See Faulkner, *Case for Greatness*; Mark A. Menaldo, *Leadership and Transformative Ambition in International Relations* (Cheltenham, UK: Edward Elgar Publishing, 2013); Haig Patapan, "Magnanimous Leadership: Edmund Barton and the Australian Founding," *Leadership and the Humanities* 4, no. 1 (2016): 1–20.

26 See David Aikman, *Great Souls: Six Who Changed a Century* (Lanham, MD: Lexington Books, 2003).

27 See Michaël de Saint-Cheron, *Gandhi: Anti-Biography of a Great Soul* (London: Taylor & Francis, 2017).

28 See Wilfred Attenborough, *Churchill and the 'Black Dog' of Depression: Reassessing the Biographical Evidence of Psychological Disorder* (New York: Palgrave Macmillan, 2014); and Joshua Wolf Shenk, *Lincoln's Melancholy: How Depression Challenged a President and Fueled His Greatness* (New York: Houghton Mifflin Harcourt, 2006).

such persons that makes their excellences remarkable. Why few individuals excel at virtue and seem to deserve the appellation great-souled is both a gift and mystery of our human condition. Aristotle stood in wonder of such human beings, and he had the recipe of thoughts and words to articulate what greatness of soul is. Greatness of soul is the characteristic that anchors all of the other virtues, puts them in good order, and presents them as a harmonious and splendid whole. Just like good archeologists, we will try to excavate the remnants of this perfect gentleman, with an eye to not only understanding who the great-souled man is, but also drawing lessons from this idea for leadership.

Greatness of soul

For Aristotle, greatness of soul is the first summit of the virtues. It is a heightened awareness that a person has reached this peak. The great-souled man wears his virtue on his sleeve because he is a supreme force of nature as regards virtue; he cannot be otherwise. But, if such a person does exist, who can share in the mind's eye of the great-souled man? The average person cannot walk in his shoes, feel as he does, and think what he thinks. How can the understanding of a modern individual without greatness of soul bridge the distance between this atypical human being and himself?

We suggest that Aristotle's discussion of the great-souled man, although only about five pages in length, has the elements of a complex and enigmatic stage character. In this way, the virtue of greatness of soul is different than any other in the *Ethics*. The reader draws away from thinking about virtue to projecting his imagination onto a concrete image. With the mind's eye, one follows the curious trail of dispositions and actions of the great-souled man. Like a good storyteller, Aristotle is playful with his main character and garnishes the great-souled man with observations that can seem a lot like off-hand expressions of the philosopher's conceits. Without the aid of a linear exposition, Aristotle forces his readers to judge where they ought to dig deeper and think about the meaning of greatness of soul. How we apply this method while attempting to keep our fanciful interpretations in check requires a brief explanation.

In this age of postmodern philosophy and literary deconstruction, the presumption is that there is no objectivity, perception is the reality, and beauty is in the eye of the beholder. No such notions exist in Aristotle's philosophy, however; the subject–object distinction is part of our vocabulary, not his. Consequently, we argue that all of the great-souled man's characteristics are subject to observation. Nothing lies in the deeper recesses of this man's unconscious psyche. We must think of his inward and exterior characteristics all in one go. Accordingly, we treat all the little accouterments that

Aristotle observes about the great-souled man as eminently meaningful, and it is with an eye to these details that we draw our composite sketch and criticisms.

According to Aristotle, it makes no difference whether we discuss the characteristic or person, so we also make no distinction between greatness of soul and the great-souled man. Aristotle's great-souled man's sense of worth emanates from a concern with honor: "[i]t is especially with matters of honor and dishonor, then, that a great-souled man is concerned" (1124a5–6). Even this man cannot altogether dispense with external validation. [He is just like us!] It is common to experience the feelings of self-worth as existing on an emotional pendulum, swinging back and forth between a personal source of esteem or the dependence upon something relational.

Many people find themselves in the grip of a relational form of external validation. Take, for example, the over-achieving student whose sense of worth is tied to grades; the playwright who hangs on the word of the critics; or the politician who brooks no criticism from the press. Each one of these hypothetical people would profit if they could only derive their sense of worth from their inherent value, at least as contemporary psychology is concerned. If only they could dispense with the need for external validation, then they might just become healthier and happier.

The great-souled man, by contrast, is immune to these common problems of self-worth, since he, Aristotle says, "deems himself worthy of great things and *is* worthy of them" (1123b2–3). Nor do his concerns with external validation compromise his inherent sense of worth. Even though he is concerned with honors, he is not tripping over himself to win acclaim. Instead, he takes pleasure in the highest honors in a measured way, and accepts them only from those that come from serious people (1124a6–7). The great-souled man's sense of worth is unshakeable because it always refers back to his greatness, and, at the same time, there is no honor worthy of complete virtue.

Like an elegantly tailored suit, the great-souled man's sense of worthiness for great things fits him just right. The same is true of those people who cut a beautiful figure. Aristotle observes that beautiful people possess the appropriate height and build, "great stature." By contrast, small people "may be elegant and well-proportioned but not beautiful" (1123b8–10). Aristotle's example of external beauty alludes to the physical and psychological structure of the great-souled man. A little later in the text, he notes that greatness of soul seems to be like a kind of ornament (*kosmos*) of the virtues (1124a1). When we hear the word ornament, we immediately think of decorations, tinsel on a Christmas tree. But Aristotle's use of this word does not imply merely an aesthetic accessory or dressing.

The word *kosmos* gives us our English word "cosmos." The Greeks, according to the seventeenth-century bishop, Isidore of Seville,

> adopted a term for world derived from "ornament," on account of the diversity of elements and the beauty of the heavenly bodies. They call it *kosmos*, which means "ornament," for with our bodily eyes we see nothing more beautiful than the world.[29]

Isodore's visible and poetic tapestry of the world includes atoms, the sky, air and clouds, thunder and lightning, the rainbow, winds and waters, seas, oceans, the abyss, and rivers. Isidore and the ancient Greeks did not separate each of the physical elements but understood them as parts of the wholeness of nature.

Subsequently, Aristotle says, "[f]or this reason, it is difficult, in truth, to be great-souled, for it is not possible without gentlemanliness (1124a2)." The gentleman, *kalokagathia*, literally "nobility and goodness," is *the* exemplar of the moral virtues.[30] The root word, *kalos*, has a range of meanings: noble, beautiful, fair, and fine. The Greeks participated in the cult of beauty and sought to imbue everything around them with beauty. They did not consider beauty as a separate domain; it was not a cultural phenomenon that one gazes at while making their way through a museum exhibit. Instead, the Greeks walked alongside beauty; it was a participant in their everyday life. Moreover, it was a civilizational milestone that they discovered that beauty resided in nature, as a law onto itself. The Greeks wrote and spoke beautifully and wrought it out skillfully in their works. If the Greeks lacked the subject–object distinction, then what was their aesthetic experience, and what relationship did it have to their view of morality?

The experience of *kalos* is something noble and beautiful, and it first comes to sight as an appearance that shines for us. It is through the eye that one must first perceive *kalos*, not as a thought but as a distinct form or image. Modern empiricism has a different starting point: our senses gather stores of data from objects to which we apply labels or names. Beautiful is

---

29 Isidore of Seville, *The Etymologies of Isidore of Seville*, trans., with intro. and notes Stephen A. Barney, W.J. Lewis, J.A. Beach, and Oliver Berghof (Cambridge: Cambridge University Press, 2006), 271.

30 Naturally, the term "gentleman" is culturally loaded, and contemporary scholarship conceives of the perfect gentleman as a social and cultural construct. Instantly, the modern imagination is populated with the image of the English gentleman or the American Southern gentleman, each with its own particular code of conduct and ethos. The Greek word Aristotle uses for gentlemanliness is: *kalokagathia*, literally "nobility and goodness." We argue that it is a notion that needs to be understood on its own terms, so we will render it as "nobility and goodness" throughout this chapter.

a broad category under which, according to personal taste, many objects are grouped. Instead, the experience of *kalos* lies in its particularity; each image is distinct and only comes to light under the right circumstances. Human sight and the object of perception are only half of the equation, as *kalos* also depends upon the human passion, which is attraction. The experience of *kalos* is equal parts of an interactive experience, human desire, and the unveiling of the image itself.

For the Greeks, our pining after *kalos* lies dormant and ascends out from the darkness into the light. The desire is woken by the sight of the splendid characteristics of beautiful objects, each one particular and perfect in itself.[31] Nature is bountiful in this regard: a starlit sky, a crescent moon, a sunset, a crystal lake, the cherry blossom. The human face is also something beautiful, and the bloom of youth makes it uniquely so. Art provides beautiful things, and even useful works can be beautiful. In a world imbued with beautiful things, morality itself dons a beautiful form in *kalokagathia*. We see this idea continue even into Christendom since a knight's shining armor means to add to the splendor of a young man's nobility and heroic virtue.

Near the end of his discussion of the great-souled man, Aristotle mentions beauty once more. He describes the gentleman's possessions: "[h]e is such as to possess beautiful and useless things *more* than useful and beneficial ones, for this is the mark of a self-sufficient person (1125a11–13, emphasis added)." The great-souled man surrounds himself with things that remind him of his virtue and worth. An abundance of useful and beneficial objects is the mark of a needy person. The more this man possesses useless things, the less he is reminded of his needs. Although Aristotle notes that he is not free from utility altogether; he has more of the useless things than useful ones. In this way, Aristotle silently qualifies his remark about the great-souled man's self-sufficiency.

The great-souled man's inner sense of worth projects itself outward by the way he looks, acts, talks, and by what he seeks out and does not seek out. Aristotle adds elements of grandeur to the great-souled man's personification: "[a]lso, slowness of movement seems to be the mark of a great-souled man, as well as a deep voice and steady speech for he who is serious about few things is not given to hastiness" (1125a13–15).

The great-souled man is like a lion, a massive cat that spends most of his time slumped in the shade – unimpressed by just about everything. There is the occasional low rumbling roar, but even then, he does not bother getting up. The lioness does all the hard work. She is the useful one that he depends

31 See Ronald Schenk, *The Soul of Beauty: A Psychological Investigation of Appearance* (Lewisberg, PA: Bucknell University Press, 1992).

upon for his uselessness – a fact he would rather forget. Only when the stakes are high, for example, a rival that threatens his pride, does he stir into action and is willing to gamble his life away.

Like the big cat, the great-souled man finds only a few things that are worthy of his attention and concern. What is there left for an utterly virtuous person to do? No proving ground tempts him. He knows himself and has a proper reverence for himself. As such, he is indifferent to other goods, such as wealth and political power, and good fortune. Turns of bad luck do not grieve him too much (1124a13–15). He even loses interest in the external good he values most since "he is not disposed even toward honor as though it were a great thing" (1124b10–11). He tends to forget about benefactions done for him while he remembers the benefactions he performs for others. When he does rise to action, it is for something momentous, like a great danger, "and when he does so, he throws away his life, on the grounds that living is not at all worthwhile" (1124b8–10).

The great-souled man makes a rare appearance. He honors a few things and does not like a crowded field. For the most part, he waits in the wings, unless "a great honor or a great deed is at stake" (1124b24–25). What compels this person's ambition toward only great things? It cannot be on account of his vanity since Aristotle is clear that along with smallness of soul, vanity is a vice, and greatness of soul is the virtue. It is the virtue that resides in greatness, which is also why the great-souled man cannot be humble. Humility is a bad fit for him, and so he is ironic with the majority of people, which is appropriate since most people find him arrogant (1124b28). With everyone else, he is truthful and open, but he does not mean to please others. The great-souled man does not pay compliments, he holds others in contempt and is not willing to live for anyone else, unless it is for a friend (1125a1). The size of this man's coterie is anyone's guess.

What is the payoff for the person to whom honor is a small thing and who is scarcely motivated to lead others, is deemed arrogant, and admires little, "since nothing is great to him" (1125a3–4)? Near the end of his account of greatness of soul, he turns to the vices and places more emphasis on smallness of soul than vanity. The small-souled person fails to capture the good things he deserves because he does not deem himself worthy of good things (1125a20–21). He does not see the identity between himself and the good things he deserves, and as a result, "he is ignorant of himself" (1125a23–24).

By contrast, the great-souled man respects himself and is the manifestation of his self-knowledge. But he is not primping himself for a ball. If such self-knowledge is good for him, is it also good for others? It strengthens the great-souled man's motivation toward virtue, which is why the steeplechase for honors holds little interest for him. And, "[h]e who is truly great-souled, therefore, must be good, and what is great in each virtue would seem to belong to the great-souled man" (1124b19–20). Although the great-souled man has scarce needs, he does eagerly want to be of service. He is not made of stone, and so the great-souled man needs an outlet to exercise his virtue. What is the payoff for everybody else? He may seem like a jerk in many respects, but the great-souled man is the most capable person in leading others.

Aristotle clarifies the leadership role of the great-souled man in the *Eudemian Ethics*. In this text, he notes that greatness of soul attaches importance to great offices. The most important honor that society confers is its highest political office, "for by investing a citizen with its supreme authority, the community entrusts him with its most precious interests" (1232b20–25). As a great-souled leader, he can use virtue and take part in great deeds. Greatness of soul is the synthesis of this man's virtue and leadership.

A word of warning about our conclusion: greatness of soul is not a theoretical model that we are trotting out as the next panacea for leadership studies. There is no textbook approach – construct model, add people – to becoming a great-souled leader. The constellation of factors, both biographical traits and historical circumstances that give rise to such people, are never in our control. Abraham Lincoln, Nelson Mandela, Martin Luther King Jr., and Mahatmas Gandhi attest to the dazzling nature of the emergence of great souls.

A great-souled leader, when they have appeared on history's scene and, if such people manifest again, is something that we need the appropriate language to disclose. To articulate our thoughts in plainspoken language is still in our power. In a world of academic jargon, polluted political language, and toxic information, there is little clarity or concreteness. Engaging with the idea of greatness of soul really encourages us to seek out the qualities and virtues that Aristotle outlined over 2,000 years ago. It is up to our readers to decide for themselves if any person can still possess them. If they judge that such virtues still exist, then such a discovery provides faith to the idea that leadership and the conduct of human affairs has a moral core. We think that in our application of this idea to Nelson Mandela, in Chapter 5, the reader will exchange with Mandela's capacious soul and kindle in their minds and hearts some correspondence with greatness.

Alexander the Great

But before coming to this more recent case study of Mandela – and before we turn the page on Aristotle – it can be illuminating to take a brief look at a case that was much closer to Aristotle's own world: the aforementioned Alexander the Great, whom Aristotle served as a tutor. Now, some modern scholars disagree whether the history of their relationship is accurate and, even if it is, to what extent Aristotle's ideas genuinely informed Alexander's own concept of leadership.[32] Yet this connection to Aristotle was well established in the scholarly tradition closer to Alexander's own time. The biographer and moralist Plutarch, for example, tells us that Philip sent for Aristotle, "the most learned and most celebrated philosopher of his time," so as to nurture the extraordinary intellectual talents of his son. He also says that

> Alexander received from [Aristotle] not only his doctrines of Morals and of Politics, but also something of those more abstruse and profound theories which these philosophers . . . professed to reserve for oral communication to the initiated, and did not allow many to become acquainted with.

Plutarch's view, in other words, is that Aristotle did not hold back from discussing some of his deepest ideas with his famous student.[33]

Despite the general contours of Alexander's life being relatively well-known, it can be useful to note a few of the high points here. Alexander (356–323 BC) was the precocious son of Philip II, king of Macedon. He distinguished himself as a leader in war at a very young age, successfully putting down revolts as a teenager in the country of Trace, to the south of Macedon, and serving at his father's side to consolidate Macedonian control over most of the cities of Greece. Alexander assumed the title of king at the age of 20, after the death of Philip, and swiftly began the gargantuan

---

32 Consider, e.g., Anton-Hermann Chroust, *Aristotle: New Light on His Life and on Some of His Lost Works*, vol. 1 (New York: Routledge, 2015), 125–32. Contrast this, however, with Joanne B. Ciulla, "Aristotle (384–322 BCE)," in *Encyclopedia of Leadership*, ed. George R. Goethels, Georgia J. Sorenson, and James MacGregor Burns (Thousand Oaks, CA: SAGE, 2004), 43–4. Ryan Balot makes an interesting comment about the connection between the two men: "It is possible to read Aristotle's *Politics*, particularly Books 7–8, as providing political recommendations for Alexander's organization of the new poleis [i.e., cities] of the East." See Ryan K. Balot, *Greek Political Thought* (Malden, MA: Blackwell Publishing, 2006), 267.

33 Plutarch, *Plutarch's Lives*, vol. 2, *The Dryden*, trans., ed. with preface Arthur Hugh Clough (New York: The Modern Library, 2001), 144. For additional thoughts on the relevance of Alexander for current models of leadership, see David Deverick, "Alexander the Great (356–323 BCE), King of Macedonia," in *Encyclopedia of Leadership*, ed. George R. Goethels, Georgia J. Sorenson, and James MacGregor Burns (Thousand Oaks, CA: SAGE, 2004), 16–20; and Barry Strauss, *Masters of Command: Alexander, Hannibal, Caesar, and the Genius of Leadership* (New York: Simon and Schuster, 2012).

task of expanding his dominion. After quelling revolts throughout his territory closer to home in Greece, he crossed the Hellespont, the narrow straits
dividing Europe from Asia, into the territories of Asia Minor in 334 BC.
There he famously is said to have planted a spear into the soil, to indicate
his forceful claim over all of Asia.[34] Through both military force and diplomacy, Alexander overtook such diverse areas of the world as Egypt and
Syria, before moving against King Darius III, leader of the Achaemenid
Empire based in Persia, or roughly the territory of present-day Iran. After
several major battles against Darius and the subsequent death of the Achaemenid leader, Alexander took complete control of the Persian Empire.
He moved to conquer lands as far east as India but found comparatively
less success in this area of the world, so remote from his native country.
Alexander died of illness at the age of 32 in the Persian capital of Babylon,
after having taken control of most of the known world and spreading Greek
culture throughout it.[35]

One of Alexander's most famous comments about his early life is that
he considered Aristotle to have been a second father to him, for "as he had
received life from the one, so the other had taught him to live well."[36] This
statement, along with our broader investigations in this chapter, raise the
question: to what extent can we say that Alexander the Great truly embodied Aristotle's teaching on character, specifically on *megalopsychia*? For
Aristotle's teaching, as we have already seen, is that living well requires living in accordance with the virtues. Was Alexander great-souled or not? And
regardless of the answer to that question, what might his example tell us
about how Aristotelian character ethics can speak to our theoretical understanding and practice of leadership?

It would be hard not to notice that many stories of the youthful Alexander
display his surpassing sense of honor and elevated self-esteem. In other
words, he appears to have viewed himself as worthy of great things to an
exceptional degree. After discussing Alexander's "temperance" and "moderation" in regard to bodily pleasures, which he demonstrated even in his

---

34 Another such indication is the famous story of Alexander cutting the Gordian Knot in the
Phrygian city of Gordium, in Asia Minor. Untying the knot was a puzzle that could be
solved only by the future "king of Asia." Alexander cut through the knot with his sword –
an indication of his willingness to use force to secure his claim to kingship of all of Asia.
[Plutarch, *Plutarch's Lives*, 152 reports another possibility: "Aristobulus tells us it was easy
for him to undo (the knot), by only pulling the pin out of the pole, to which the yoke was
tied, and afterwards drawing off the yoke itself from below."]
35 Scholars of ancient history and politics note that one of Alexander's great successes was
spreading Greek culture through the wider world. See, e.g., Balot, *Greek Political Thought*,
266–9; and Strauss, *Masters of Command*, 6.
36 Plutarch, *Plutarch's Lives*, 145.

youth, Plutarch says that he was very eager in his "love of glory," showing a "solidity of high spirit and magnanimity far above his age." Whereas his father Philip appeared to desire victory and glory always and for any reason, Alexander valued these things if, and only if, the activities that earned him victory and glory were worthy of him. For instance, when asked if he would like to run races in the Olympic games, Alexander is said to have replied yes, but only "if he might have kings to run with him."[37] In the epic battle of Gaugamela, "the greatest battle that Alexander and Darius would ever fight," in the words of the historian Barry Strauss,[38] the advisors of Alexander tried to convince their leader to attack Darius at night. The Macedonian king, however, responded in a manner that seems nothing if not magnanimous, saying "I will not steal a victory."[39]

Even the generosity of the mature Alexander seems indicative of the attitude of *megalopsychia*, and perhaps displays for us how this particular virtue serves as the crown of all of the rest – generosity being an essential virtue in Aristotle's moral philosophy. Aristotle notes that the great-souled man is "the sort to benefit others but is ashamed to receive a benefaction; for the former is a mark of one who is superior, the latter of one who is inferior" (1124b9–11). According to Plutarch, Alexander was always "munificent" in his life, but he "grew more so as his fortune increased, accompanying what he gave with that courtesy and freedom which, to speak truth, is necessary to make a benefit really obliging." One would expect, of course, that taking control of the vast riches of Persia would allow Alexander to practice the virtue of liberality more frequently and to a much greater extent. But we also learn that Alexander "was always more displeased with those who would not accept of what he gave than with those who begged of him."[40] In other words, his preference was to be the benefactor, as that was a sure sign of his superiority. Any indication from followers that his gifts were not needed was, by contrast, a sign that others had attained the superior standing.

But what are we to make of the fact that Alexander's life was doggedly devoted to one goal, namely rulership of the whole world? One may say a great many things, both positive and negative (depending on one's perspective), about Aristotle's great-souled man. Does it seem right, however, to call him an imperial force and to see *megalopsychia* as consistent with

37 Plutarch, *Plutarch's Lives*, 141–2.
38 Strauss, *Masters of Command*, 107.
39 Plutarch, *Plutarch's Lives*, 165. He most certainly did not "steal" this victory: see Strauss's full analysis of Alexander's leadership in military tactics at Gaugamela (109–19).
40 Plutarch, *Plutarch's Lives*, 170–1.

empire? Another aspect of Alexander's soul that is impossible to miss is his all-consuming ambition, or love of superiority and the renown that goes along with it. A mark of high ambition is an intense drive to succeed – a clear attribute of his, as Alexander "was not easily to be diverted from anything he was bent upon."[41] He sought difficult tasks as a proving ground for this drive. For instance, as a youth, he wished to avoid inheriting a stable dominion from his father Philip, preferring instead "a kingdom involved in troubles and wars" because he knew that political instability would provide the opportunity to cement a name for himself. And when firmly in command of his whole empire, having become king of Asia, Alexander exhibited an ardently intense love of glory. He took to wearing the opulent clothing of Persia, and to showering his friends and followers with money, material goods, and power. We learn from Plutarch that, in due time, Alexander lost his level-headedness in conversation with others and, instead, began to lash out "when anybody spoke ill of him . . . valuing his glory and reputation beyond his life or kingdom."[42]

There seems to be, then, something else going on here in the moral experience of Alexander the Great. Now, Aristotle's formal discussion of ambition as a virtue falls directly on the heels of his discussion of greatness of soul. These two treatments are intimately related, as both of these virtues concern honors – although ambition, by contrast with *megalopsychia*, seems to cover "measured and small things" (1125b5). The peculiar aspect of Aristotle's discussion of ambition, however, is that he is unable to name the virtue (as the mean) and vices (as the two extremes) using plain, differentiated language. Common opinion speaks of the moral phenomenon using relative terms and ideas: there is a "lack of ambition," for example, when people seem habitually to eschew honors even when they are noble, yet somebody might be blamed as "ambitious" when he seeks to acquire honor from the wrong places or in the wrong ways. In other words, the experience of moral individuals reveals such ambiguities to the intelligent observer when it comes to matters of honor.

Our reading of the case of Alexander the Great, to conclude, indicates that one can expect to find certain similar ambiguities in the moral experience of leaders concerned with honor. Stated another way, Alexander shows that it can sometimes be very difficult to distinguish between true greatness of soul and mere ambition – this latter term understood more so as a vice than as a virtue – in our leaders. Alexander most definitely understood himself to be worthy of great things, but this sense of self, and all that goes

41 Plutarch, *Plutarch's Lives*, 160.
42 Plutarch, *Plutarch's Lives*, 173–4.

along with it, as we have seen in Aristotle's explanation of the virtue, tended to slip into the intensely passionate love of renown rather easily. And if our reading of Nelson Mandela's life in Chapter 5 is accurate, then we should be all the more impressed by the character and moral leadership of the father of South Africa. Before we get there, we turn to our third and final philosophic text, Niccolò Machiavelli's *The Prince* – an explosive book on leadership that operates very much outside of the ethical perspective that we have seen in Aristotle.

Bibliography

Aikman, David. *Great Souls: Six Who Changed a Century*. Lanham, MD: Lexington Books, 2003.

Aristotle. *Aristotle's Nicomachean Ethics*. Translated, with an Interpretive Essay, Notes, and Glossary, by Robert C. Bartlett and Susan D. Collins. Chicago: University of Chicago Press, 2011.

Aristotle, and H. Rackham. *The Athenian Constitution: The Eudemian Ethics: On Virtues and Vices*. Cambridge, MA: Harvard University Press, 1967.

———. *The Rhetoric and the Poetics of Aristotle*. Translated by W. Rhys Roberts and Ingram Bywater. New York: Modern Library, 1984.

Attenborough, Wilfred. *Churchill and the 'Black Dog' of Depression: Reassessing the Biographical Evidence of Psychological Disorder*. New York: Palgrave Macmillan, 2014.

Balot, Ryan K. *Greek Political Thought*. Malden, MA: Blackwell Publishing, 2006.

Bartlett, Robert, and Susan Collins. "Introduction." In Aristotle, *Aristotle's Nicomachean Ethics*, translated, with an Interpretive Essay, Notes, and Glossary, by Robert C. Bartlett and Susan D. Collins, vii–xiv. Chicago: University of Chicago Press, 2011.

Bowman, James. *Honor: A History*. New York: Encounter Books, 2007.

Brock, Roger. *Greek Political Imagery from Homer to Aristotle*. London: Bloomsbury Publishing, 2013.

Brooks, David. *The Road to Character*. New York: Random House, 2015.

Brown, Ryan P. *Honor Bound: How a Cultural Ideal Has Shaped the American Psyche*. New York: Oxford University Press, 2016.

Cabrera, Luis. *The Humble Cosmopolitan: Rights, Diversity, and Trans-State Democracy*. New York: Oxford University Press, 2019.

Cantor, Paul A. *Pop Culture and the Dark Side of the American Dream: Con Men, Gangsters, Drug Lords, and Zombies*. Lexington: University of Kentucky Press, 2019.

Chroust, Anton-Hermann. *Aristotle: New Light on His Life and on Some of His Lost Works*. Vol. 1. New York: Routledge, 2015.

Ciulla, Joanne B. "Aristotle (384–322 BCE)." In *Encyclopedia of Leadership*, edited by George R. Goethels, Georgia J. Sorenson, and James MacGregor Burns, 43–4. Thousand Oaks, CA: Sage Publications, 2004.

Cohen, John Alan. *The Primitive Mind and Modern Man.* Sharjah, UAE: Bentham Science Publishers, 2010.

Conney, Mark. *Honor Cultures and Violence.* New York: Oxford University Press, 2013.

Deverick, David. "Alexander the Great (356–323 BCE), King of Macedonia." In *Encyclopedia of Leadership*, edited by George R. Goethels, Georgia J. Sorenson, and James MacGregor Burns, 16–20. Thousand Oaks, CA: Sage Publications, 2004.

Faulkner, Robert K. *The Case for Greatness: Honorable Ambition and Its Critics.* New Haven, CT: Yale University Press, 2007.

Henderson, Katherine U., and Barbara F. McManus. *Half Humankind: Contexts and Texts of the Controversy about Women in England, 1540–1640.* Champaign: University of Illinois Press, 1985.

Isidore of Seville. *The Etymologies of Isidore of Seville.* Translated, with Introduction and Notes, by Stephen A. Barney, W.J. Lewis, J.A. Beach, and Oliver Berghof. Cambridge: Cambridge University Press, 2006.

Johnson, Laurie M. *Honor in America?: Tocqueville on American Enlightenment.* Lanham, MD: Lexington Books, 2016.

Landy, Marc, and Sidney M. Milkis. *Presidential Greatness.* Lawrence: University Press of Kansas, 2000.

Lewis, C.S. *Mere Christianity.* New York: Simon and Schuster, 1996.

Melzer, Arthur M. "Character vs. Free Will: Aristotle and Kant on Moral Responsibility." In *In Search of Humanity: Essays in Honor of Clifford Orwin*, edited by Andrea Radasanu, 435–48. Lanham, MD: Lexington Books, 2015.

Menaldo, Mark A. *Leadership and Transformative Ambition in International Relations.* Cheltenham, UK: Edward Elgar Publishing, 2013.

Merritt, James. *Character still Counts: It Is Time to Restore Our Lasting Values.* Eugene, OR: Harvest House Publishers, 2020.

Patapan, Haig. "Magnanimous Leadership: Edmund Barton and the Australian Founding." *Leadership and the Humanities* 4, no. 1 (2016): 1–20.

Pinker, Steven. *The Better Angels of Our Nature: Why Violence Has Declined.* New York: Penguin, 2012.

Plutarch. *Plutarch's Lives, Volume II.* The Dryden Translation. Edited with Preface by Arthur Hugh Clough. New York: The Modern Library, 2001.

Saint-Cheron, Michaël de. *Gandhi: Anti-Biography of a Great Soul.* London: Taylor & Francis, 2017.

Schenk, Ronald. *The Soul of Beauty: A Psychological Investigation of Appearance.* Lewisberg, PA: Bucknell University Press, 1992.

Shenk, Joshua Wolf. *Lincoln's Melancholy: How Depression Challenged a President and Fueled His Greatness.* New York: Houghton Mifflin Harcourt, 2006.

Sommers, Tamler. *Why Honor Matters.* New York: Basic Books, 2018.

Sousa, Milton, and Dirk van Dierendonck. "Servant Leadership and the Effect of the Interaction between Humility, Action, and Hierarchical Power on Follower Engagement." *Journal of Business Ethics* 141, no. 1 (2017): 13–25.

Strauss, Barry. *Masters of Command: Alexander, Hannibal, Caesar, and the Genius of Leadership*. New York: Simon and Schuster, 2012.

Tocqueville, Alexis de. *Democracy in America*. Translated, Edited, and with an Introduction by Harvey C. Mansfield and Delba Winthrop. Chicago: University of Chicago Press, 2000.

Tucker, Shawn R. *Pride and Humility: A New Interdisciplinary Analysis*. New York: Palgrave Macmillan, 2016.

4 Machiavelli

Radical realism and the morally flexible leader

Niccolò Machiavelli, one of Italy's great Renaissance thinkers and writers, was born in Florence in 1469. His father Bernardo, a lawyer by training, was held in esteem and was an amateur scholar. The Machiavellis were a respectable middle-class family, but they did not command either power or wealth. Little is known about Machiavelli's early life. It is not until his political debut at the age of 29 that his biographical information becomes available, mostly through his penning of copious letters. Florence's broader political history matters in Machiavelli's life, however, as it framed his entry into politics.

In the centuries leading up to the fifteenth, the Florentine Republic grew into one of Italy's five great city-states. Although Florence adopted a constitution limiting political office and tenure, in reality, influential merchant and banking families dominated the corridors of political power. Among these families, the Medicis carved out supreme influence in the city. The creators of the Medici Bank, the most powerful of its kind in the fifteenth century, the Medici used their powers and riches to create a political dynasty and bankroll Renaissance artists and writers.

The Medici gained control of Florence in 1434 when Cosimo de' Medici triumphantly returned from exile and he, in turn, exiled the city's other leading families. The Medici commanded the loyalty of powerful Florentine families through the use of patronage. In the year of Machiavelli's birth, Lorenzo de' Medici, known as Lorenzo il Magnifico, assumed power. Lorenzo presided over Florence during its golden age and acted as the fulcrum of Italy's balance of power and the principal patron of the city's artists, architects, and writers. When Lorenzo died in 1492, his son Piero de' Medici, known as Piero the Unfortunate, owing to his lack of political judgment, assumed control of Florence, but his tenure lasted only 2 years. When Charles VII of France invaded Italy with vastly superior forces, Piero made a bargain with the king that cost him his throne. Piero voluntarily gave up key territories in return for an alliance with France. The loss of Pisa, especially, aroused the anger of Florentine citizens, who then sacked the Medici Palace and exiled Piero in 1494.

The end of the Medici reign ushered in a real republican government, and Machiavelli entered the political stage by gaining employment as the Second Chancellor of the Republic. As the secretary to the Republic's Council, a governmental body of amateurs that rotated office every 2 months, he took on wide-ranging diplomatic responsibilities and became Florence's roving ambassador. For Machiavelli, the experience was a monumental one; his job exposed him to the art and practice of statecraft. Moreover, not being a dignitary himself, and representing a militarily weak Florence, which relied on France's troops for its defense, he was always negotiating from a position of weakness. During his tenure as a civil servant, he was the architect of Florence's citizen militia. It is no surprise that the idea of the force of arms as the cornerstone of political power became one of the central themes of his political thought.

Machiavelli served the Republic faithfully between 1498 and 1512. In his first diplomatic mission, he went to France for a 7-month stay in the French court in 1500–1501. In 1502, he went on a mission to the Romagna, where he became intimately acquainted with Cesare Borgia, otherwise known as Duke Valentino. At the time, Cesare was leading a Papal Army in the name of his father, Pope Alexander VI, and was conquering vast portions of the Romagna and Marche, while "fomenting rebellions among Florence's subject city-states."[1] Cesare figures prominently in Machiavelli's letters and writings and seems to have inspired many of the princely qualities that have become synonymous with Machiavellianism. Consequently, we discuss the military and political career of this warrior prince in this chapter, especially how Cesare illustrates Machiavelli's radical moral reasoning.

Machiavelli's political career ended when the Medici family overthrew the Florentine Republic and restored itself as the ruling dynasty. The Medici regime soon dismissed him from his job as secretary, and within a year he was implicated in a conspiracy, which he was most unlikely a part of, to overthrow the Medici. He was arrested and tortured for 3 weeks. A change in political circumstances would come to Machiavelli's aid while in prison. The death of Pope Julius II led to Cardinal Giovanni de' Medici's ascension to the papal chair, who took the name of Leo X. In an act of clemency, the new pope released all political prisoners, and Machiavelli was set free.

Jobless and out of favor with the Medicis, Machiavelli left the city to live at his country farm in Sant'Andrea in Percussina. He did not enjoy country life, as rural inhabitants were not suited to his temperament: a skilled diplomat with a keen intellect. Yet, it was in this state of political indolence that Machiavelli combined his experience in state affairs and long-study of

---

1 John T. Scott, *The Routledge Guidebook to Machiavelli's the Prince* (London: Routledge, 2016), 7.

ancient thinkers and wrote the most famous and the most infamous book on politics ever written, *The Prince*.

The Prince and its influence

Writing to his friend Francesco Vettori in 1513, Machiavelli describes that he has written a

> little work *De Principatibus* [On Principalities], where I delve as deeply as I can into reflections of this subject, debating what a principality is, of what kinds they are, how they are acquired, how they are maintained, why they are lost.[2]

The book is part tract, part treatise. It is also short and dedicated to Lorenzo de Medici. Like many books in this genre, Machiavelli seeks to ingratiate himself with the city's ruler. At first glance, *The Prince* seems like a petition for employment that is thin on substance.

In truth, *The Prince* is not merely a job application nor a shallow account of political maneuvering. As Machiavelli confessed to Vettori, he spent "all his time fattening and polishing it" (*L*). He also made sure to distribute the work to his friends first, for fear that Medici's secretary, Ardinghelli, would claim it as his own. Machiavelli's concerns were well placed: *The Prince* was radically innovative, and it had a profound influence on the study of political philosophy and political life.

Machiavelli influenced Francis Bacon, Thomas Hobbes, John Locke, Jean-Jacques Rousseau, and America's founding fathers. For example, concerning American Democracy, some of Machiavelli's central tenets are built into its constitutional framework.[3] The Federalist Papers, the most famous exposition of the Constitution, assumes that human beings are self-interested and that morality is not the end of politics. Instead, the machinery of government is a reflection of human nature and meant to control human passions rather than elevate human beings to a higher purpose. Princely ambition is the core conflict that the separation of powers is meant to solve, as Publius famously says, in Federalist Paper No. 51, "ambition must be

2 This letter (Niccolò Machiavelli to Francesco Vettori, Florence, December 10, 1513, translated by Harvey Mansfield) appears in the appendix to Mansfield's translation of *The Prince* that we have used. See Niccolò Machiavelli, *The Prince*, 2nd ed., trans. and with an intro. Harvey C. Mansfield (Chicago: University of Chicago Press, 1998). In our parenthetical text references, page numbers citing the works of Niccolò Machiavelli appear as follows, Letter to Francesco Vettori (*L*), *The Prince* (*P*) and *Discourses on Livy* (*D*).
3 See C. Bradley Thompson, "John Adams's Machiavellian Moment," *The Review of Politics* 57, no. 3 (1995): 389–417.

made to counteract ambition." Moreover, the executive consolidates power into one person, and this official is given discretion to act decisively, especially in emergencies.

Although Machiavelli is not a core figure in contemporary leadership studies, his ideas are especially relevant. What scholars call situational approaches are a clear reflection of Machiavelli's insights.[4] Keith Grint gets closest to understanding the chameleon-like leadership style of Machiavelli's prince, as he describes the need for situational leaders to use a "repertoire of styles to suit the particular situation."[5] In Grint's view, Machiavelli belongs in a group of classical thinkers of leadership, among Plato and Sun Tzu. For the most part, Machiavelli is ignored by leadership scholars because he is an obstacle to the humanist and ethical normativity that directs contemporary leadership theory.

The question for leadership studies, as Joanne Ciulla has noted, is not "What is leadership?" but "What is good leadership?"[6] The latter implies something both moral and effective. Machiavelli would add that good (effective) leadership sometimes requires that leaders behave badly.[7] Nevertheless, leadership scholars and readers must contend with Machiavelli because his ideas are arguably the reason why leadership studies is consumed with theories of moral elevation and authenticity.[8]

There are many wide-ranging interpretations of *The Prince*.[9] Still, there is an overarching consensus that Machiavelli's work not only departs

---

4 See Kenneth H. Blanchard, Drea Zigarmi, and Robert B. Nelson, "Situational Leadership® after 25 Years: A Retrospective," *Journal of Leadership Studies* 1, no. 1 (1993): 21–36; Barney Glasser and Anselm Strauss, *The Discovery of Grounded Theory* (Chicago: Aldine Publishing Co., 1967); and Robert P. Vecchio, "Situational Leadership Theory: An Examination of a Prescriptive Theory," *Journal of Applied Psychology* 72, no. 3 (1987): 444–51.

5 Keith Grint, *Leadership: Classical, Contemporary, and Critical Approaches* (Oxford: Oxford University Press, 1997), 5.

6 Joanne B. Ciulla, *The Ethics of Leadership* (Belmont, CA: Wadsworth/Thomson Learning, 2003), xii.

7 Notable among leadership scholars is Barbara Kellerman who recognizes not only the need to study bad leadership, but also the nuanced place that we ought to reserve for Machiavelli in our discussion of this topic. See Barbara Kellerman, *Bad Leadership: What It Is, How It Happens, Why It Matters* (Cambridge: Harvard Business Press, 2004).

8 See generally Brent Edwin Cusher and Mark A. Menaldo, eds., *Leadership and the Unmasking of Authenticity: The Philosophy of Self-Knowledge and Deception* (Northampton, UK: Edward Elgar, 2018).

9 See Harvey C. Mansfield, *Machiavelli's Virtue* (Chicago: University of Chicago Press, 1996); J.G.A. Pocock, *The Machiavellian Moment: Florentine Political Thought and the Atlantic Republican Tradition* (Princeton, NJ: Princeton University Press, 2016); Leo Strauss, *Thoughts on Machiavelli* (Chicago: University of Chicago Press, 2014); and Maurizio Viroli, *Redeeming the Prince: The Meaning of Machiavelli's Masterpiece* (Princeton, NJ: Princeton University Press, 2013).

from the philosophical and literary forms of its time, but also ushers in the main principles of modernity. In *The Prince*, Machiavelli makes sweeping claims about human nature and morality, while also providing a unique understanding of the interplay of power, fortune, and necessity. At the core of Machiavelli's new perspective is his demand to examine "what is done" (realism) in public life rather than "what ought to be done" (idealism). Machiavelli offers his readers a frank and unapologetic political realism.

Princely politics is a game of chess, and every move is for the sake of winning. In politics, everything depends upon circumstances. Like a chess strategy, a prince must adapt his political strategy to the changing facts on the ground. Machiavelli relaxes general ethical rules and undermines the view that a leader must possess distinct and unbending character virtues. Freed from constraints of principled leadership, a prince practices tough-minded politics for the sake of dominion (holding on to his state). Deception, which entails a clear-eyed understanding of why and when a leader deceives, is necessary for the prince to maintain his state. The prince seeks solid foundations between himself and followers, not authentic or ethical ones.[10] The view that emerges in the book is that public life subsumes a prince's life: the acquisition and maintenance of the state. For Machiavelli, it is all about the means, and it is what *The Prince* is ostensibly famous for, "ends justify the means" – although Machiavelli did not actually write this phrase. What he actually says is,

> in the actions of all men, and especially of princes, where there is no court to appeal to, one looks to the end. So let a prince win and maintain his state: the means will always be judged honorable, and will be praised by everyone.
>
> (*P* 18)

Through shrewd calculation, coloring his nature (deception), and being bad when it serves his good, the prince makes the appropriate use of *virtù*.

From the Latin word, *virtus*, and the ancient Greek word, *arēte*, Machiavelli takes the classical and Christian notions of moral virtue and makes them his own. By neglecting righteousness and conscience, Machiavelli reduces the problem of leadership and politics to social dependence, and limiting this dependence is of primary concern to a prince. In other words,

---

10 Mark A. Menaldo, "Leadership and the Virtue of Deception in Niccolò Machiavelli's *The Prince*," in *Leadership and the Unmasking of Authenticity: The Philosophy of Self-Knowledge and Deception*, ed. Brent Edwin Cusher and Menaldo A. Menaldo (Northampton, UK: Edward Elgar, 2018), 90–112.

he is locked in an infinite game of political relationships and must energetically keep his place on the ladder of political relationships – which is on top. What governs his rise or fall is either his fortune (luck) or his virtue (*virtù*). Virtue is in a prince's control, while fortune is not. This view may seem uncontroversial from a modern reader's perspective who ascribes to the adage, "you make your own luck." But if it were not for Machiavelli, such a belief and attitude might not have ever come into existence.

Machiavelli's nimble mind and consummate writing skills were matched by his grand ambition to initiate a wholesale transformation in philosophy. He effectively accomplished this feat by splitting philosophy into two camps, which we will refer to for our purposes here as realists and idealists. Machiavelli is the founder of political realism.

From classical antiquity to the Christianity practiced in Machiavelli's day, idealism reigned. Ancient philosophers, such as Aristotle, premised their arguments that the good life was the ideal and was also intelligible to human beings through reason. These philosophers were keen to distinguish between art, convention, and nature. And they viewed the thoughts, choices, and practices of human beings as the sources of art and convention, while nature stood alone, and was not subject to change. The discovery of nature by Greek philosophers introduced the notion of an independent and persistent reality, and lent support to the idea that reasonable discourse about politics and morality could improve society. Philosophers hoped that if and when people understood ethical standards according to reason, rather than mere emotional attachments to convention, human beings would live according to virtue in a well-ordered political society. As Plato's Socrates outlines in the *Republic*, and as we showed in Chapter 2, the rule of philosopher-kings would finally put the squabbling for honor and power to rest.

Following Greek thinkers, Christian theologians assumed that a higher natural law existed, but God, not nature, was the source of this eternal law. What ancient and natural law philosophers shared in common was the idea that moral codes admitted of an objective source. By contrast, speaking as a Christian, St. Augustine argued that political life – the temporal City of Man – could never fulfill the human soul because a person's true home was with God. It was best for a person to prepare for God's kingdom, the eternal City of God.

The force behind idealism did not relent in Machiavelli's time. In the humanist climate of Renaissance Florence, there existed a strong desire to infuse ancient ideas and cultural ideals into religious practice, which showed the enormous credibility and staying power of the idealism and notions of the good life. This classical spirit walked side by side in politics, as the good life provided a blueprint for princely rule. During the Renaissance, the well-established genre mirror for princes advised these leaders to pursue monarchical ends while practicing cardinal virtues.[11]

In 1516, 3 years after Machiavelli wrote *The Prince*, Desiderius Erasmus published *The Education of a Christian Prince*. Through artful rhetoric, Erasmus invoked the wisdom of the pagan philosophers while keeping true to the Christian faith. He recommended piety, humility, and policies of peace, above all else. When Machiavelli set to work on *The Prince*, he knew well that he was defying not only the classical tradition, but also the Christian pieties that were obligatory for an author to mention in a manual for princes. Yet Machiavelli was bent, as he later voiced in his *Discourses on Livy*, his major tome on politics, on embarking on "a path yet untrodden by anyone" (*D* I.1).[12]

Machiavelli's untrodden path

The Prince is Machiavelli's opening volley for this untrodden path. Not only does Machiavelli forge the distinction between idealism and realism, but also he prepares his readers for a new direction in leadership. To illustrate these ideas, we have selected to analyze, in full, the central passage in *The Prince* where Machiavelli contrasts the real and ideal and radically redefines the ethics of leadership. This passage is also the most famous in *The Prince*, so we have chosen to reproduce it at length. In the opening paragraph of Chapter 15, entitled "Of those things for which Men and Especially Princes are Praised and Blamed," Machiavelli says:

> It remains now to see what the modes and government of a prince should be with subjects and friends. And because I know that many have written of this, I fear that in writing of it again, I may be held presumptuous, especially since in disputing this matter I depart from the orders of others. But since my intent is to write something useful to whoever understands it, it has appeared to me more fitting to go directly to the effectual truth of things than to the imagination of it. And many have imagined republics and principalities that have never been seen or known to exist in truth; for it is so far from how one lives to

11 For an extensive bibliography, see Roberto Lambertini, "Mirrors for Princes," in *Encyclopedia of Medieval Philosophy*, ed. Henrik Langerlund (New York: Springer Publishing, 2011), 791–7.
12 We have used the following translation of Machiavelli's *Discourses*: Niccolò Machiavelli, *Discourses on Livy*, trans. Harvey C. Mansfield and Nathan Tarcov (Chicago: University of Chicago Press, 1996).

how one should live that he who lets go of what is done for what should be done learns his ruin rather than his preservation. For a man who wants to make a profession of good in all regards must come to ruin among so many who are not good. Hence it is necessary to a prince, if he wants to maintain himself, to learn to be able not to be good, and use this and not use it according to necessity.

[*P* 15]

In previous chapters of *The Prince*, Machiavelli had given princes, especially new ones, guidance on how to acquire and retain their states. Later, in our chapter, with the example of Cesare Borgia, we will review some of this guidance. In the opening sentence of Chapter 15, Machiavelli turns to the treatment of subjects and friends. In a subtle hint of what is to come, Machiavelli tells his readers that there will be more than one mode (*modo*) to deal with subjects and friends.[13] Aristotle, in his text *The Politics*, classified regimes by the terms aristocracy, timocracy, oligarchy, democracy, and tyranny. Machiavelli only speaks of republics and principalities, yet also seems to blur these two into a single notion, which is the state. And to rule a state, a prince can make use of many modes, which resemble regime types.

In the next few sentences, Machiavelli introduces an idea that marks a monumental shift in the history of philosophy and political thought. First, he quickly puts aside his initial misgivings about broaching a subject that others have written upon because he claims to depart significantly from these writers. These writers, namely philosophers, have worn out this matter and are merely repeating the same ideas, but Machiavelli is going to say something new about an old subject. He warns his readers that he may be held presumptuous. While this can mean that what he says may seem arrogant, it can also mean that he will fail to observe the limits of what is permitted or appropriate. Machiavelli, we believe, is stressing both meanings of the word presumptuous.

Machiavelli's departure from the writings of others depends upon his abrupt and unequivocal dismissal of all previous thought. Admittedly, this is a sign of arrogance. He describes philosophy as a constellation of utopias and fictions that exist only in the imagination. The imagined republics and principalities of thinkers such as Plato and St. Augustine are fanciful because there is no ordinary experience of such phenomena. There is no philosopher kingship on record except in Plato's *Republic*, and until Christians see the vision of God in heaven, they must hold on to the lamp of faith.

---

13 Erica Benner, *Machiavelli's Prince: A New Reading* (New York: Oxford University Press, 2013), 179.

In place of these naïve ideas, Machiavelli claims that he will go "directly to the effectual truth of the thing." The phrase, effectual truth (*verità effettuale*), which Machiavelli coins, might sound unimpressive to our contemporary ears. The binding of fact to utility anticipates modern epistemology and science's evidence-based approach to reality. Modernist sensibilities prime today's readers to assume that "to see is to believe." Yet, in what follows, we unpack Machiavelli's phrase and show how it contains his revolutionary ideas about politics, morality, and leadership. Through such an analysis, we demonstrate that his prediction will become true, by testing the limits of conventional thought in a way no one ever has, and that we should rightfully hold him to be presumptuous.

Writing almost a century before Galileo's discoveries, Machiavelli's effectual truth is the primary thrust engine of modernity. From Machiavelli's perspective, classical philosophy seals itself off from reality and, because it exists in the imagination, renders itself useless. What is a useful philosophy? That which is given to observation. One might retort, "but looks can be deceiving." And since Socrates, philosophy is bound by the quest to separate appearances from that which truly exists. For Machiavelli, this distinction, the bread and butter of philosophy, led philosophers astray. Truth is a matter of utility and not borne from the fanciful metaphysical talk about ultimate reality.

What is Machiavelli's stance on appearance and reality? The effectual truth, or utility, is the ultimate judge. If an appearance produces something useful, then that perception is the reality. Reality follows appearance, and through this idea Machiavelli reverses the direction of philosophy. Here we can begin to see the subversive character of Machiavelli's ideas for not only his time but also its impact on the future. Machiavelli's effectual truth collapses the distinction between perception and reality, which is the harbinger of the postmodern notion that truth is simply a matter of perspective. Yet Machiavelli is not interested in merely deconstructing philosophy's sacred cows; he puts this insight about the effectual truth in the service of a prince's needs, which is to build and maintain solid foundations for his leadership. A prince, we shall see, must learn how to deftly use qualities that are perceived by followers as moral characteristics, and use them as circumstances demand.

By casting aside philosophy as imaginative (idealism), and introducing the effectual truth (realism) in its place, not only does Machiavelli render philosophy sober, he also upends moral conventions about human behavior. Following his point about imagined republics and principalities, he qualifies his statement with what seems like a simple and uncontroversial statement of fact: "for it is so far from how one lives to how one should live." Machiavelli seems to be saying that the idealists are far off the mark because they refuse to see human nature for what it is. How human beings live out their ordinary lives *is* human nature. Machiavelli has already summed up his view of human nature earlier in the book: "and truly it is a very natural and ordinary thing to acquire" (*P* 3).

Acquisitive and needy, are these the basic characteristics of human beings, and is there nothing else? A bleak outlook. No wonder idealist notions of a transcendent human good dominated philosophy and religion for so long, since they speak to intense longings at the core of human experience: a better life for oneself and one's descendants, community, and country. An idealist must remain hopeful, but Machiavelli thinks such misplaced hopes lead to people forgetting necessity and human nature. A prince who is susceptible to high hopes needs the cooling effect of Machiavelli's realism. Returning to the passage in Chapter 15, he warns a prince: "that he who lets go of what is done for what should be done learns his ruin rather than his preservation." Hope is a dangerous political delusion; Machiavelli's adds no gauze to comfort his readers.

In life and politics, hope brings comfort and sustains our notions of the good life (what should be done). For example, ancient idealists understand that chaotic elements in human nature make people unrestrained and unruly. Still, classical philosophers think governance ought to make people better. Through proper education, the human soul can be tuned and harmonized through the cultivation of intellectual and moral virtues – such as in the case of Aristotle's ethical philosophy, which we analyzed in the previous chapter. Living a virtuous life is one way to attain the good and seek happiness. For Christians, original sin is the cause of people suffering difficulty, pain, and death. While there was no remedy for life in the flesh, the hope of salvation is offered by God's redemptive project, in Jesus Christ's deliverance from sin and its consequences. In both cases, ancient and Christian, people hold out hope that there is more to life than self-serving behavior and that virtue coupled to a transcendent good will protect against the vicissitudes of fortune.

Machiavelli offers no succor to the hopeful and barely mentions justice in *The Prince*. Thus, we can infer that when he says that the prince will learn his ruin rather than his preservation, he means that bad things will eventually happen to those who try to mind the gap between the "ought" and the "is." While the idealist tradition renders self-preservation as the baser part of human nature, Machiavelli sees self-preservation as the epicenter on which life turns, and its truth is in plain sight because it is rooted in necessity.

The righteous, who "want to make a profession of good in all regards, will come to ruin," because they live in a world where people are, for the most part, not good (*P* 15). A prince cannot put his faith in other people or God while also staying well attuned to the fear of ruin and desire for preservation.

For Machiavelli, human beings are on their own; there are no transcendent or divine supports coming to their aid. This idea is in marked contrast with what Paul the Apostle says in his epistle to the Romans (8.28): "And we know that in all things God works for the good of those who love him, who have been called according to his purpose."

Self-preservation is essential when a new prince assumes power. Changes in leadership plant the seeds for an unsatisfied followership; some will be unhappy that a leadership change did not vault them into a higher position than they expected. Others still will chafe under a new prince, in their belief that they themselves possess the mettle to be a prince. For a new prince to preserve his state and avoid ruin, Machiavelli concludes the first paragraph by supplying a general rule of princely conduct: "hence it is necessary to a prince, if he wants to maintain himself, to learn to be able not to be good, and to use this and not use it according to necessity" (*P* 15).

This rule seems easy enough to understand. Following a hard-boiled perspective, a layman might say, "look out after yourself even if that means you need to get your hands dirty."[14] But the familiar sense misses the layered meaning in Machiavelli's general rule. To learn how not to be good, a prince must forgo all his conventional attachments, including his identity, by undergoing a moral reversal. A prince has to rid himself of conscience, a deeply ingrained sense of right and wrong that seems to be an outcrop of anthropological development across all human cultures. Despite the variability of cultures and moral codes, morality seems coeval with society, and moral conscience with consciousness. By asking a prince to cast away his collective and personal moral memory, Machiavelli is guiding a prince to see past morality and culture. Instead, the prince must have an uncanny sense of the primordiality of man by being attuned to necessity, which is the root of human behavior.

Continuing in text, and "leaving out what is imagined about a prince," Machiavelli says that he will focus on what is true. He then lists all the notable qualities that matter for a prince, which are those that bring him praise or blame (*P* 15). The qualities include:

> liberal and mean; giver and rapacious; cruel and merciful; breaker of faith and faithful; effeminate or pusillanimous and fierce or spirited; human and proud; lascivious and chaste; honest or open and

---

14 According to Terry Price, leaders "are said to get their hands dirty when, for the sake of what might be called a 'higher cause,' they engage in behavior that is generally thought to be morally wrong." Terry L. Price, "Dirty Hands," in *Encyclopedia of Leadership*, ed. George R. Goethels, Georgia J. Sorenson, and James MacGregor Burns (Thousand Oaks, CA: SAGE, 2004), 338–40. See also Terry L. Price, *Leadership Ethics: An Introduction* (New York: Cambridge University Press, 2008), 149–50.

astute or cunning; hard and agreeable; grave and light; religious and unbelieving.

(P 15)

What should we make of Machiavelli's list? The casual reader might glance at these qualities and move on, but these pairs, with no additional explanation from Machiavelli, are central to his reclassification of moral language.

On the surface, each quality appears as a virtue, followed by its contrary vice. But this presentation should already give a reader pause. Machiavelli calls these "qualities," which is a term that makes its first appearance here in *The Prince*, and it suggests a psychological disposition and capacity. The use of the word quality also blurs the categorical difference between virtue and vice.[15] Machiavelli's rapid listing of these qualities raises the question: what does each quality consist of? For example, are liberal and mean mutually exclusive capacities or, in fact, one quality – a composite of virtue and vice? If they are a composite of opposite pairs, then virtue needs its corollary vice to stand out. Each coin has two sides. When followers recognize a prince's virtues or his vices, it is because they speak about him in terms of praise and blame. If people praise a prince for being liberal, then he is not being blamed as mean. A prince is showcasing the composite quality liberal and mean in such a way to elicit this praise. A prince must be artful in his demonstration of a quality because he will always be either praised or blamed. Recognition for his virtue is a glossy finish while being blamed for vice is the result of dullness.

Machiavelli's discussion of the general rule and possession of qualities reminds us of the putative Elizabethan phrase, "we princes . . . are set on stages, in sight and in view of the world." Machiavelli's prince is an actor, and he must manage the stage on which he appears by avoiding the infamy of vices that would lead him to lose his state, while, with "less hesitation," he should practice vices that could help him gain and keep his state. Since the crucible of leadership is how others perceive him in terms of good and bad, Machiavelli tells the prince that he "should not care about incurring the fame of those vices without which it is difficult to save one's state." For Machiavelli, a good prince is effective at controlling the moral climate that enables his ascendance and maintenance of power.

How does a new prince become a Machiavellian leader? Machiavelli indicates that a prince must consider "everything well," so leadership

---

15 Clifford Orwin, "Machiavelli's Unchristian Charity," *American Political Science Review* 72, no. 4 (1978): 1218.

depends on learning. And it seems that Machiavelli shows a prince that there are two overarching lessons. First, the reality of virtue and vice is that they are merely appearances that matter only in their practical consequences. The prince must understand the connection between appearance and outcome, but especially be ready to apply this lesson in the hardest cases, when virtue results in a prince's ruin and vice results in his well-being. The second, and seemingly harder, lesson is that a prince needs to internalize this reality so that he can break bad. A prince must learn to get past feelings of shame and act shamelessly, because, in reality, nothing is shameful. At the same time, Machiavelli advises the prince to avoid a particular shame (*infamia*), the infamy of vices that lead him to the ruin of his state. A notoriety for vices that lead to the dispossession of the state is an effectual truth that is bad. Subsequently, if a prince holds on to his state, he will be praised and gain a good reputation. Success or failure are the effective lenses that filter peoples' perception of virtue and vice.

But there is even a more profound lesson for the leader (prince) who considers "everything well." We argue that this person who understands Machiavelli's teachings is one who understands how necessity coincides with the human being's natural vulnerability. From birth, human beings have no special dispensation from nature and live in perpetual uncertainty because fortune works independently of their desires and hopes. Necessity teaches that nature is both indifferent and chaotic; hence, human order has to be imposed. This order consists of one discernible end for a human being, which is his self-preservation, and self-help is the only reliable source for survival. Existential and psychological vulnerability marks the human journey from the cradle to the grave. The person who considers "everything well" is in touch with this primordial aspect of human life and sees the evidence of it in the formation of political communities.

From the very beginning of *The Prince*, Machiavelli focuses on the challenges faced by a new prince who has no natural claim to rule, builds on uncertain foundations, and wrestles dramatically with fortune. The full scope of Chapter 15, Machiavelli seems to suggest, is that the prince may need to use unmitigated harshness when particular circumstances call for actions beyond the pale. It is not very different from what a person would do if they were left alone to fend for themselves in the so-called natural condition where life, according to Thomas Hobbes, in the famous description from his *Leviathan*, is "solitary, poor, nasty, brutish, and short."[16]

---

16 Thomas Hobbes, *Leviathan, with Selected Variants from the Latin Edition of 1668*, ed. with intro. and notes Edwin Curley (Indianapolis: Hackett Publishing, 1994), 76.

The new prince that emerges in *The Prince* is, in a qualified sense, a transcendent figure. He overcomes the tendency of being lulled into complacency by false comforts and hopes, and never forgets necessity. As we shall see next, faith in others is one of these false comforts and hopes. A true prince depends on no one and alone plumbs the depths of primordial necessity. By walking a path untrodden by others, Machiavelli takes potential leaders down a path that one can only travel in solitude.

Machiavellian *Virtù* in practice: Cesare Borgia, duke of the Romagna

Liberality

In Chapter 16, Machiavelli explains the first quality that matters for a prince: liberality and parsimony (the giving and spending of money).[17] The prince, Machiavelli comments, should never be liberal because followers cannot recognize liberality. In fact, followers only think a prince is liberal when he spends on them in excess (by effectively practicing prodigality). To seem liberal in the eyes of followers, the prince always has to spend more. What Machiavelli is describing in this chapter is the psychology of entitlement. When a prince gives to his followers he might be thanked for his giving, but, in time, followers will presume that what they receive from a prince is their just deserts and will see no reason to reciprocate by showing gratitude. Subsequently, simply to appear liberal a prince must become prodigal, and eventually exhaust his resources.

Liberality is an effectual bad because, by spending everything he has on followers, the prince must use up his own money or tax the people. Taxes are loathsome and lead to resentment. To be deemed liberal, a prince, Machiavelli argues, should be stingy. The prince should never spend any money because by doing so he will avoid the infamy of "a name for meanness," which is when one spends but then pulls back on spending (*P* 16). If he never gives, his followers will start to believe that he is generous because the prince is not burdening them with taxes or dispossessing them of their property. But a prince must make war, and this costs money. War presents the prince with an altogether different set of challenges. Necessity compels him to practice liberality/prodigality with his soldiers. In war, a prince worries less about spending because he fills his war chest by employing booty, pillage, and ransom.

---

17 In the *Nicomachean Ethics*, Book III, Aristotle identifies liberality as a virtue and parsimony and prodigality as vices.

Cesare Borgia's army was essentially a mercenary army, which was composed of troops on loan from Louis the XII and of Italians led by captains known as *condottiere*. Representing powerful Roman families, such as the Orsini and Colonna, the *condottiere* were notoriously fickle and risk-averse. Cesare initially won success with these troops, but he understood that his dependence on both mercenary soldiers and the will of the French king stood in the way of his desire to become the dominant prince of Italy. In *The Prince*, Machiavelli discusses Borgia's worry about the risks of using mercenaries. He had availed himself of the Orsini soldiers and had sensed their lack of aggressiveness when he tried to attack the city of Bologna. At the same time, King Louis XII stopped Cesare Borgia from attacking Tuscany after he had brilliantly seized Urbino, a medieval walled city in Le Marche (Northwest Italy).

After these two incidents, Machiavelli says, "[h]ence the duke decided to no longer depend on the arms and fortunes of others" (*P* 7). He weakened his rivals in Rome, the Orsini and Colonna, by paying the "gentlemen" (*gentili uomini*) of these families higher pay and giving them rank and title in his court (*P* 7). By lavishing them with these beneficences, Cesare made the men forget the factional disdain between these two groups, and "all affection turned toward him" (*P* 7). He did not stop a liberality, however; his next ploy was to try and destroy the Orsini and Colonna, which we take up in our discussion of deception.

Cruelty well-used

In Chapter 17, Machiavelli first observes convention. He says it is better to be thought merciful and not cruel. But a prince who is known for cruelty well-used is even better because it may alleviate an unruly body politic. Mercy often leads to moral hazard by allowing "disorders to continue." Machiavelli's Italy was a miserable place in terms of law and order, which was especially true of the Papal States. The Romagna, which figures significantly in *The Prince*, was run by tyrannical warlords who did not recognize the Church's authority and subjected citizens to intolerable acts of terror. Machiavelli did not endorse such despotic rule, which is why he calls it "disorder." In his eyes, these tyrants were not only small-minded but made themselves hated.

Machiavelli then makes a segue into one of his most famous observations – and one with very clear leadership implications. He says, "from this a dispute arises, whether it is better to be loved than feared, or the reverse" (*P* 17). The answer is that it is best to be both feared and loved but since it is not entirely possible to have both, a prince should leverage fear. Moreover, Machiavelli thinks that love is unreliable, and in politics, love is a mere spectacle. Followers shower the prince with praise and promises: "while you do them good, they are yours, offering you their blood, property, lives, and children" (*P* 17). Only in the instant that a person makes a promise to another does the bond (oath) seem unbreakable. But commitment begins to wane the moment after a follower pledges his love. If a prince relies on love, he is dependent on a "chain of obligation, which because men are wicked is broken on every opportunity for their own utility" (*P* 17).

The prince's optimal choice is to depend on fear since it "is held by the dread of punishment that never forsakes you" (*P* 17). Machiavelli concludes the chapter by saying that people "love at their convenience and fear at the convenience of the prince" (*P* 17). How can a prince establish a proper relationship with followers based on fear? He needs a reputation for cruelty that does not hurt the political community at large, but uses singular examples. And, for Machiavelli, Cesare Borgia excelled in the art of cruelty well-used. In Chapter Seven of *The Prince*, Machiavelli goes out of his way to describe Cesare's gift for this dramatic vice. In the first part of the chapter, he summarizes the events that led to Cesare's consolidation of the tumultuous cities of the Romagna. He then singles out one event in particular that he says he does not want to leave out because other aspiring princes ought to imitate Borgia in this regard.

The Romagna, a region in Northeastern Italy, was poorly governed. The tyrannical warlords who held power over its towns had many times beat back Papal armies that sought to take control of the region. In 1500, Cesare Borgia's army began a conquest of the region by taking the cities of Forli and Imola. He then installed Remirro de Orco (Ramiro de Lorqua) as governor of the Romagna, who governed it from 1501–1502. De Orco was one of Borgia's Spanish born captains, a weathered veteran of the Iberian Crusades, who Machiavelli describes as a "cruel and ready man" (*P* 7). Borgia gave him full power to oversee the region, and de Orco proceeded to bring unity and peace to the previously lawless Romagna, while also gaining "a great reputation for himself" (*P* 7).

But de Orco became known for the zealous and high-handed manner in which he executed his duties. Borgia worried that the peoples' satisfaction with peace and unity could quickly turn into hate. In October 1502, Borgia created a civil court where each city of the Romagna had a representative. Then on Christmas morning of that same year, the townspeople of Cesena awoke to find de Orco "in two pieces, with a piece of wood and a bloody knife beside him" (*P* 7). Machiavelli stresses the effect this act had on the people: "the ferocity of this spectacle left the people at once satisfied and stupefied" (*P* 7).

How could such a spectacle satisfy anyone? Speaking for Borgia, Machiavelli says that "because he knew that past rigors had generated hatred for

Remirro, he wished to show if any cruelty had been committed, this had not come from him but from the harsh nature of his minister" (*P* 7). De Orco's murder separates the peoples' hatred for de Orco from Borgia and helps purge their spirits. After a long period of disorder and de Orco's firmness, the people have earned a respite. By cleansing their anger toward de Orco, they feel that justice is done – even if done unjustly. Yet, how was this spectacular punishment stupefying? The people of the Romagna had seen either the same or even worse during its long lawless history. Yet such violence and disorder were rooted in petty vendettas or wanton acts of aggression. In the case of de Orco, there was no trial or public explanation for the act. The mystery and silence surrounding de Orco's execution might be interpreted as Borgia's use of arbitrary justice, but, instead, we argue it had a purpose. Shrouded in mystery, the violent execution against de Orco seems to defy conventional notions of justice. Despite their satisfaction, the witnesses are left to wonder, "did de Orco deserve to die?" They cannot answer this question because de Orco was Borgia's trusted lieutenant, and he had served him well. Borgia's power is awe-inspiring: de Orco was sacrificed, and they were spared. This act of redemption extends Borgia's claim over the life and conduct of the people. They will be grateful now and in the future because they are free of disorder and Borgia, they realize, chooses to remit punishment against them. For these reasons, it would seem that Machiavelli believes Borgia's cruelty is a princely quality worthy of imitation.

Returning to Chapter 17, Machiavelli ties Borgia's dramatic act to his notion of cruelty well-used. In this chapter, Machiavelli observes that mercy enables disorder to continue, which produces murders and robberies. A prince might try to suppress this lawlessness by casting a dragnet, but such means can become oppressive and hurt the whole community, leading to hatred toward the prince. One singular execution, however, "hurts one particular person." Borgia's pacification of the Romagna and execution of de Orco is the real-world application of Machiavelli's paradigm of cruelty well-used.

Faith and astuteness: the lion and the fox

In Chapter 18, Machiavelli contrasts living by faith with astuteness. While faith means living with integrity and trust in others, astuteness makes use of guile and cunning. Machiavelli first praises faith but quickly observes that astute princes readily take advantage of those who live by faith. There is nothing revelatory about Machiavelli's observation; it is common for honest and trusting people to be taken advantage of by their opposites. In what then seems like a non-sequitur, Machiavelli changes direction and says, "you must know that there are two kinds of combat: one with laws, the other with force." Machiavelli has drawn parallels in this initial antithetical set-up: on one hand, there are faith and astuteness, and, on the other hand, law and force. As we shall argue, however, this is a rhetorical sleight of hand by Machiavelli. These two seemingly antithetical modes of combat, law and force, will reveal a prince's need to live astutely by draping himself in a cloak of faith. Subsequently, force articulates itself in law. In essence, this chapter reveals Machiavelli's formula for the virtue of deception.

Machiavelli says that law is fit for human beings, and force is for beasts. He observes that mere law is not sufficient for ruling, so a prince needs to make use of force. Enforceable law is, of course, the reality of law, but Machiavelli separates the two notions. The use of force requires knowledge; the prince, Machiavelli says, needs to "know how to well" use the beast and man (*P* 18). So where can a prince learn how to use force? Machiavelli says that a prince must turn to the concealed teachings in covert writings for this lesson. Ancient writers taught the knowledge of the beast and man, but they hid their lessons in images. For example, antiquity's greatest hero, Achilles, was raised by Chiron the centaur. For Machiavelli, Chiron symbolizes "that a prince needs to know how to use both natures; and one without the other is not lasting" (*P* 18). In Chapter 14, Machiavelli says that Achilles is worthy of imitation: "Alexander the Great imitated Achilles." Although Aristotle's influence on Alexander was paramount, as we discussed in Chapter 3, Alexander must have also absorbed these covert teachings regarding the beast and the man from another source. Machiavelli's single reference to an ancient author and text in *The Prince* is to Xenophon and his *Education of Cyrus* (*P* 14).

Machiavelli proceeds to use his own images to render the covert teaching overt. To "know how to well" use the beast, he says that a prince should choose the fox and the lion because lions cannot avoid snares (traps), and foxes do not defend themselves from wolves (*P* 18). Foxes can recognize pitfalls, and lions can scare off wolves. But princes, Machiavelli emphasizes, should not stick with the lion at the expense of being foxlike. The fox is the superior animal; moreover, it symbolizes Machiavellian prudence (knowledge) or practical wisdom. And, returning to the thesis of Chapter 18, Machiavelli says, "a prudent lord cannot observe faith."

He justifies this prescription by noting that not all men are good, and those who are wicked will not observe faith with the prince, so the prince is justified in not keeping faith with them. By implication, a prince will be the same with the wicked and good, since a prince does not observe faith. Practical wisdom makes no effort to discern between good and bad character. A prince blankets all his dealings with others with deception. Consequently, a prince's practical wisdom is motivated by a single end, which is to come out on top: "the one who has known best how to use the fox comes out best" (*P* 18).

The mode of the fox denies what seems like a necessary convention of human life, and especially leadership, which is that honest dealing and building trust is paramount. Machiavelli would agree, but a prince must feign such honesty: "it is necessary to be a great pretender and dissembler" (*P* 18). Machiavelli is not making a case here for pathological lying, a condition of narcissism and sociopathology. Deception is an art that enables a prince to color his nature for the sake of winning in this highest of stakes game, which is political life. For Machiavelli, a prince's political survival has no guarantees, and in light of a loss of his power, he may also lose his life.

Consequently, the prince that emerges here is not a cruel sociopath. Instead, a prince is an exuberant actor, and his mode is finding ways to beguile his friends and subjects alike.[18] To attract these two types to himself and succeed in leadership, he must wear many masks. Machiavelli says that the prince must seem "all mercy, all faith, all honesty, all humanity, all religion. . . . So let a prince win and maintain his state: the means will always be judged honorable, and will be praised by everyone" (*P* 18).

Both Cesare and his father, Pope Alexander VI, were eminently foxlike. Machiavelli says that the Pope "never did anything, nor ever thought of anything, but how to deceive men" (*P* 18). Regarding Cesare's virtue of deception, we must return to the end of Chapter Seven, where Machiavelli states all of the Duke's accomplishments and lauds him for his ferocity and virtue. Cesare's ferocity, we had seen, was rooted in his ability to be ruthless when the circumstances demanded. Not only did he execute his trusted lieutenant, Ramirro de Orco, but he also eliminated the heads of families who had served in his military campaigns. Yet, when Cesare made use of his lion-like ferocity, it was only in light of carefully orchestrated deceit and dissimulation. The cornerstone of Cesare's virtue was the concealment of his intentions. Although Machiavelli does not go into depth about Cesare's use of deception against the family heads in *The Prince*, the Duke's story illustrates the lesson of the beast and the man.

In October 1502, Cesare's captains called a secret meeting in Rome. They had become increasingly suspicious of his intentions to aggrandize himself, which seemed to go far beyond the conquest of Romagna. Among those in attendance in the meeting was Gianpolo Baglioni. He warned all in attendance that if they did not rise against the Duke, they risked being "devoured

---

18 We remind the reader that the first sentence of Chapter 15 advises the prince how to deal "with subjects and friends."

one by one by the dragon."[19] Since 1499, many family heads and captains in attendance had made war alongside Cesare, but after the meeting, they committed to fight against him. Once news of this conspiracy spread throughout Italy, it led to uprisings against Cesare in cities that recently had lost their independence to the Duke's army.

These conspirators were ruthless tyrants in their own right; each had used force and terror to keep their territories and power. They included Giaonpolo Baglioni of Perugia, Oliverotto Eufreducci of Fermo, Pandolfo Petrucci of Siena, and Paolo and Cardinal Orsini of Rome. Cesare's secretiveness and deception were critical for him to survive the conspiracy. Intending to return to the field of conquest, Cesare began to strike deals with individual conspirators. Marred by indecisiveness and defections, the scheme foundered. Cesare bought off the conspirators, one by one, with small bribes.[20] In return, the conspirators would stop stoking the uprisings, give him back control of strategic cities in the Romagna, and add to his war chest.

Surprisingly, Cesare did not exact any punishment on the captains. By returning to the status quo, the lenient Cesare had reconciled with each of them. Or so it seemed. On their part, the captains were happy to be useful to him and served him in military matters to show their renewed loyalty. With the conspiracy subdued, Cesare sent three generals, Paolo Orsini, Vitelozzo Vitelli, and Oliverotto Eufreducci, ahead to the city of Senigallia to suppress it and make ready for Cesare.

As we previously discussed, with no explanation and no trial, Cesare arrested and then executed Ramirro de Orco. The day after this execution, on December 26, he left Cesena, his stronghold, in the Romagna. He sent his army elsewhere and was accompanied only by his guard, a risky decision given that the plot against him was still fresh in everyone's memory. Yet Cesare was demonstrating two things to the captains by moving with a light security force. He showed to his reconciled captains that he did not fear them, and, at the same time, by not arriving with his whole army, he signaled to his generals that they also ought to feel secure. In their attempt to show good faith to Cesare, the generals went to meet him with a minimal escort when he arrived in Senigallia on December 31. By coincidence, Machiavelli was traveling with Cesare at this time and was witness to these events, which he describes in his correspondence:

> Vitellozo, Pagolo, and the Duke (Orsini) of Gravina, riding mules, went to meet the Duke, accompanied by a few cavalry. And Vitellozo, unarmed, in a cloak lined with green, very disconsolate, as though he

19 Miles J. Unger, *Machiavelli: A Biography* (New York: Simon and Schuster, 2011), 121.
20 Unger, *Machiavelli*, 126.

were aware of his coming death . . . When these three, then, came into the presence of the Duke and saluted him courteously, he welcomed them with a pleasant face . . . [Later] having entered Senigallia, all of them dismounted at the quarters of the Duke and went with him into a private room, where the Duke made them prisoners.[21]

On New Year's morning, Vitellozzo and Oliverotto were found dead from being strangled. That same day, Cesare marched his troops from Senigallia to Rome, with three Orsini as his prisoners, and they joined Cardinal Orsini in the prison of Pope Alexander VI.

Imitating Cesare and Machiavelli

Cesare achieved a meteoric rise in his short political career. He established a principality of his own, subdued the warlords of the Romagna and unified it, built the most fearsome army in Italy, and packed the College of Cardinals with loyalists. Cesare acted with zeal and vigor because the tenure of any pope was always uncertain, which is something that bore in the mind of the Duke. In 1503, when Alexander VI fell ill to an illness that he would succumb to, Cesare had no control over such an event, nor could he have foreseen the graver misfortune that befell him, which is that he also became very sick. Pope Alexander and Cesare were likely stricken by malaria.[22]

Consequently, Cesare was now a diminished figure, both physically and politically. When Pope Julius II ascended the throne, he made many promises to Cesare that he did not keep. Ousted as captain-general of the Pope's army, Cesare would have to procure money of his own to keep his army intact so that he could hold on to the Romagna. It was all for nothing. Eventually, Pope Julius II arrested and deported Cesare to Spain, and he died in battle at age 31, fighting in an inconsequential war for his brother-in-law's army of Navarre.

For Machiavelli, Cesare Borgia is a prototypical new prince that rises to power through fortune. Although Cesare acquired all his state through the assistance of Alexander VI and lost it through the same, he "laid for himself great foundations for future power" (*P* 7). Machiavelli concludes his discussion of Cesare in Chapter Seven with the following statement: he should be "imitated by all those who have risen to empire through fortune and the arms of others" (*P* 7).

---

21 Unger, *Machiavelli*, 131.
22 Gerald J. Meyer, *The Borgias: The Hidden History* (New York: Random House, 2013), 387.

If imitation is the sincerest form of flattery, then even in Cesare's failure, there is something to behold. Machiavelli's emphasis on Cesare's gruesome execution of Ramiro de Orco stands out as his most imitable act. Cesare shows his mastery of how spectacle can transform something that people with a moral conscience ought to condemn into an effectual good: an ordered political community.

Machiavelli praises imitation and he also wears many masks: the secretary, diplomat, military strategist, intellectual, citizen, and prince, in his own right. Machiavelli is the archetypical fox. To imitate means not only to aim for an accurate and realistic representation of the truth but to exaggerate or even misrepresent the truth. All artists deceive the eye and fool us; we believe we are looking at the real thing. In leadership, deception produces colorful and shocking images that satisfy and stupefy. Some people will follow the Cesares of the world; others, who have considered everything well, will imitate Machiavelli.

Bibliography

Benner, Erica. *Machiavelli's Prince: A New Reading*. New York: Oxford University Press, 2013.

Blanchard, Kenneth H., Drea Zigarmi, and Robert B. Nelson. "Situational Leadership® after 25 Years: A Retrospective." *Journal of Leadership Studies* 1, no. 1 (1993): 21–36.

Ciulla, Joanne B. *The Ethics of Leadership*. Belmont, CA: Wadsworth/Thomson Learning, 2003.

Cusher, Brent Edwin, and Mark A. Menaldo, eds. *Leadership and the Unmasking of Authenticity: The Philosophy of Self-Knowledge and Deception*. Northampton, UK: Edward Elgar, 2018.

Glasser, Barney, and Anselm Strauss. *The Discovery of Grounded Theory*. Chicago: Aldine Publishing Company, 1967.

Grint, Keith. *Leadership: Classical, Contemporary, and Critical Approaches*. Oxford: Oxford University Press, 1997.

Hobbes, Thomas. *Leviathan, with Selected Variants from the Latin Edition of 1668*. Edited with Introduction and Notes by Edwin Curley. Indianapolis: Hackett Publishing, 1994.

Kellerman, Barbara. *Bad Leadership: What It Is, How It Happens, Why It Matters*. Cambridge: Harvard Business Press, 2004.

Lambertini, Roberto. "Mirrors for Princes." In *Encyclopedia of Medieval Philosophy*, edited by Henrik Langerlund, 791–7. New York: Springer Publishing, 2011.

Machiavelli, Niccolò. *Discourses on Livy*. Translated by Harvey C. Mansfield and Nathan Tarcov. Chicago: University of Chicago Press, 1996.

———. *The Prince*. 2nd ed. Translated and with an Introduction by Harvey C. Mansfield. Chicago: University of Chicago Press, 1998.

Mansfield, Harvey C. *Machiavelli's Virtue*. Chicago: University of Chicago Press, 1996.

Menaldo, Mark A. "Leadership and the Virtue of Deception in Niccolò Machiavelli's *The Prince*." In *Leadership and the Unmasking of Authenticity: The Philosophy of Self-Knowledge and Deception*, edited by Brent Edwin Cusher and Menaldo A. Menaldo, 90–112. Northampton, UK: Edward Elgar, 2018.

Meyer, Gerald J. *The Borgias: The Hidden History*. New York: Random House, 2013.

Orwin, Clifford. "Machiavelli's Unchristian Charity." *American Political Science Review* 72, no. 4 (1978): 1217–28.

Pocock, J.G.A. *The Machiavellian Moment: Florentine Political Thought and the Atlantic Republican Tradition*. Princeton, NJ: Princeton University Press, 2016.

Price, Terry L. "Dirty Hands." In *Encyclopedia of Leadership*, edited by George R. Goethels, Georgia J. Sorenson, and James MacGregor Burns, 338–40. Thousand Oaks, CA: Sage Publications, 2004.

———. *Leadership Ethics: An Introduction*. New York: Cambridge University Press, 2008.

Scott, John T. *The Routledge Guidebook to Machiavelli's the Prince*. London: Routledge, 2016.

Strauss, Leo. *Thoughts on Machiavelli*. Chicago: University of Chicago Press, 2014.

Thompson, C. Bradley. "John Adams's Machiavellian Moment." *The Review of Politics* 57, no. 3 (1995): 389–417.

Unger, Miles J. *Machiavelli: A Biography*. New York: Simon and Schuster, 2011.

Vecchio, Robert P. "Situational Leadership Theory: An Examination of a Prescriptive Theory." *Journal of Applied Psychology* 72, no. 3 (1987): 444–51.

Viroli, Maurizio. *Redeeming the Prince: The Meaning of Machiavelli's Masterpiece*. Princeton, NJ: Princeton University Press, 2013.

5　Case studies

Case study one: Bill Gates

If one tries to imagine a prospective philosopher-king, then a mental picture might emerge of a rare bird, devoting herself to the study of perennial questions through the close reading of great books. Cogitating, not decision-making, would seem like her preferred activity, and only reluctantly choosing practical life over restful contemplation. As we noted in Chapter 2, rulership is toil and requires that the philosopher leave the sun's eternal light to return to the Cave's dark world, where reality is mere shadows. For millennia, Plato's analogy of the good inspired the promising youths of different ages and cultures to live a contemplative life.

Aristotle, Alfarabi, and St. Thomas Aquinas exemplified this approach in their lives and thoughts during the classical and medieval periods. Early moderns, such as Bacon, Hobbes, and Hume, reversed course by focusing on materialism and empiricism. The German idealist tradition provided a bulwark against British empiricism. Leibniz, Kant, and Hegel were exemplars of the Platonic notion of eternal ideas.

The incidence of philosophy comingling with leadership is rare, but some notable exceptions are worth referring to. France's philosophically inclined president, Emanuel Macron, once debated dozens of scholars and intellectuals in an 8-hour televised debate.[1] Peter Theil, the co-founder of PayPal, studied 20th-century philosophy at Stanford.[2] Pope Francis I studied philosophy and theology, as all Popes must. Yet this one, the first chosen from a Latin American country, Argentina, has fashioned a decisive stance on

---

1 Paul Cohen, "France's Philosopher-Presidents," *Dissent*, March 29, 2019, www.dissent magazine.org/online_articles/frances-philosopher-presidents.
2 Max Nisen, "9 Famous Execs Who Majored in Philosophy," *Business Insider*, January 19, 2014, www.businessinsider.com/successful-philosophy-majors-2014-1?op=1.

social justice, specifically regarding the effect of unchecked capitalism on inequality and the environment.[3]

Notwithstanding such standouts, there is little incentive for business and political leaders to cultivate philosophical habits of mind. So-called Thought Leadership shuns the solitude and pensive character needed for philosophy, although intellectual deepening would serve leaders well.[4] Instead, Thought Leadership admires influencers who are good at branding and building relationships. In a world of stiff market competition, thought leaders need to make sure their products remain distinguishable. In a world that lauds quick thinking and high-flying decision-makers, where might we find slow and deliberate thinker leaders?

We argue that Bill Gates has many markings of a 21st-century philosopher-king, although the first half of his life does not seem to admit this model. In his youth, Gates showed an insatiable curiosity for software and coding, which was matched by his boundless entrepreneurial ambition. In 1967, just 12 years old, Gates read *Fortune* magazine religiously and dreamed of launching his own company. In the eighth grade, he, Paul Allen, and a couple of friends founded the Lakeside Programming Group and offered their services to companies in return for free time to use their computers, a rare luxury in those days.[5]

At Harvard, Gates majored in applied math, studied computer science, and routinely skipped classes, choosing to audit the courses he was interested in. But his real passion was his monomaniacal obsession with launching the first company that would create software for personal computers while turning it into a profitable business. After his sophomore year, he dropped out of Harvard and joined forces with Paul Allen to found Microsoft. For Gates, the excitement of a new dawn for the tech age and the lure of succeeding in his ambition trumped the ivory tower. His dream was simple yet revolutionary for its time, "a computer on every desk and in every home."[6]

His ideas about computers and software revolutionized the world and generated immense wealth for himself and others. In the 1990s, Gates

3 Francis, *Laudato Si'* (Washington, DC: United States Conference of Catholic Bishops, 2015), 18–19.

4 See Schumpeter, "Philosopher Kings: Business Leaders Would Benefit from Studying Great Writers," *The Economist*, October 4, 2014, www.economist.com/business/2014/10/04/philosopher-kings.

5 Walter Isaacson, *The Innovators: How a Group of Inventors, Hackers, Geniuses and Geeks Created the Digital Revolution* (New York: Simon and Schuster, 2014), 312.

6 Hannah Bae, "Bill Gates' 40th Anniversary Email: Goal Was 'a Computer on Every Desk'," *CNNMoney*, April 6, 2015, https://money.cnn.com/2015/04/05/technology/bill-gates-email-microsoft-40-anniversary/index.html.

famously became the world's richest man, while his company, Microsoft, was engaged in a rivalry with Apple and became infamous for its involvement in anti-trust suits.[7] At the helm of Microsoft, people knew Gates for his ruthlessness toward competitors, while, as a boss, employees suffered from his abuse and belittling.[8] As a difficult boss bent on preserving his company's monopoly, this early portrait of Gates is hardly the stuff of a person in love with the truth. Gates says, "I was quite fanatical about work. I worked weekends, I didn't really believe in vacations."[9]

Yet, more interesting is Gates's second act, when he stepped down as the CEO of Microsoft in 2000, and his day-to-day role in 2008. Bill and Melinda launched their foundation in 2000, which helped turn Gates into a full-time philanthropist. The argument we advance here is that Bill Gates's "second-sailing"[10] from business to philanthropy requires a synthesis of the qualities of Plato's best leader, which is contemplation and action. The reasons that Bill and Melinda Gates give for beginning their foundation are simple. They are giving away their wealth because they believe it is a moral responsibility, but Bill Gates also notes that it enlists his pure joy of thinking and problem-solving.[11]

In other words, for Gates, philanthropy is compulsory. It is only just that he gives away wealth, so he and his wife, Melinda, put it to fair use through their foundation. They lead together in a co-equal partnership to fight inequities facing the world's most disenfranchised people. By liberating himself from the business world's Machiavellian climate, Gates thoroughly educates himself for the foundation's goals and for its own sake. For example, the Gates Foundation helps developed countries and farmers improve their agricultural processes. It is not enough to provide monetary aid, however, Gates thinks it is an absolute necessity to learn about the projects he backs:

> I am a little obsessed with fertilizer. I mean I'm fascinated with its role, not with using it. I go to meetings where it's a serious topic of conversation. I read books about its benefits and the problems with overusing

7 See Nell Musolf, *Built for Success: The Story of Microsoft* (Mankato, MN: The Creative Company, 2008).

8 Julie Bort, "Loved and Hated: The Life and Awesomeness of Bill Gates," *Business Insider*, May 28, 2012, www.businessinsider.com/awesome-life-bill-gates-2012-5#a-mean-unfair-software-baron-9.

9 Bill Gates, "Desert Island Discs: Bill Gates," interview by Kirsty Young, *BBC Radio 4*, February 5, 2016, www.bbc.co.uk/programmes/b06z1zdt.

10 For the significance of this term in Platonic philosophy, see Seth Benardete, *Socrates' Second Sailing: On Plato's Republic* (Chicago: University of Chicago Press, 1992).

11 Bill and Melinda Gates, "Our 2018 Annual Letter: 10 Tough Questions We Get Asked," *GatesNotes*, February 13, 2018, www.gatesnotes.com/2018-Annual-Letter.

it. It's the kind of topic I have to remind myself not to talk about too much at cocktail parties, since most people don't find it as interesting as I do. But like anyone with a mild obsession, I think mine is entirely justified. Two out of every five people on Earth today owe their lives to the higher crop outputs that fertilizer has made possible. It helped fuel the Green Revolution, an explosion of agricultural productivity that lifted hundreds of millions of people around the world out of poverty.[12]

His worldview is essentially optimistic and believes that human beings can make the world better by studying problems and applying sound reasoning. Gates's moral philosophy applies the classic utilitarian principle, "the greatest good for the greatest number."[13] In a Netflix documentary, *Inside Bill's Brain*, Gates describes his philanthropic work as "optimization," which he elaborates on in his blog:

> I describe what I do as "optimization" – a wonky way of saying I try to make sure our limited resources help as many people as possible. I'll never be the intrepid health worker on the front lines fighting disease. But if our foundation and its partners can help that worker reach more children with better tools, we all can create better lives for generations to come. Our decision to fight polio is one of the best examples.[14]

In 1988, the World Health Organization launched the Global Polio Eradication Initiative (GPEI), which reduced the virus by 99% and from 125 countries to 3. Today, polio is only found in Afghanistan, Pakistan, and Nigeria. There are not many cases reported globally, but it appears nearly impossible to completely eradicate the virus, which is highly contagious and flares up across different regions in these countries. The optimization problem, in this case, is that vaccination campaigns cost around US $1 billion per year. This creates a long-term problem, of large amounts of money chasing fewer and fewer cases of polio, without being able to accomplish the goal of complete eradication. The Gates's foundation makes a strategic commitment in these countries that couples financial and technical resources, helping funding existing campaigns such as the GPEI, while contributing to non-traditional investments and taking big risks.[15]

---

12 Bill Gates, "Here's My Plan to Improve Our World: And How You Can Help," *Wired*, November 12, 2012, www.wired.com/2013/11/bill-gates-wired-essay.
13 See John Troyer, *The Classical Utilitarians* (Indianapolis: Hackett, 2003).
14 Bill Gates, "A Bet on Humanity Worth Every Dollar," *Gatesnotes*, September 20, 2019, www.gatesnotes.com/About-Bill-Gates/A-bet-on-humanity.
15 "What We Do: Polio-Strategy Overview," Bill and Melinda Gates Foundation, accessed January 6, 2021, www.gatesfoundation.org/what-we-do/global-development/polio.

Bill Gates's philosophical optimism is steeped in deliberate thinking that depends mightily on reading. On his blog "GatesNotes" one can find an exceptional array of books that Gates has read, is reading, and recommends to others. Despite managing his foundation, Gates reads one book per week and has five simple rules to read and retain the information he reads.[16] In addition, Gates takes what he calls "think-weeks," in which twice a year, he reads, takes notes, and thinks in complete solitude at a modest clapboard cottage in the Pacific Northwest. He began this practice while at Microsoft, and continues it to this day.[17]

Gates's appetite for reading helps him find well-grounded arguments for his optimism. For example, in the 2012 book, *The Better Angels of our Nature*, and 700 pages in length, Steven Pinker argues that our era is less violent, less cruel, and more peaceful than any previous period of human existence.[18] Pinker's thesis runs counter to the prevailing wisdom that modernity has ushered in brutal warfare and totalitarian states that have done more harm than good. Have human beings become more peaceful because of the progress of reason? Gates, who firmly believes in the enhanced powers of reasoning, found Pinker's arguments so convincing that in a letter to the graduating class of 2017 (everyone earning a college degree) he said, if

> I could give each of you a graduation present, it would be a copy of *The Better Angels of Our Nature*, by Steven Pinker. After several years of studying, you may not exactly be itching to read a 700-page book. But please put this one on your reading list to get to someday. It is the most inspiring book I have ever read.[19]

It is not enough for Gates to read about the growth of human intelligence. He thinks that we can use our mental faculties to solve global problems. For example, Gates was not only vocal when the Covid-19 pandemic first hit but prophetic. In a 2015 article, written for the *New England Journal of Medicine*, Gates wrote: "we must prepare for future epidemics

16 Sam Benson Smith, "The Four Rules of Reading According to Bill Gates," *Asia Reader's Digest*, accessed January 6, 2021, www.rdasia.com/true-stories-lifestyle/thought-provoking/four-rules-reading-according-bill-gates.

17 Robert A. GuthStaff, "In Secret Hideaway, Bill Gates Ponders Microsoft's Future," *The Wall Street Journal*, March 28, 2005.

18 Steven Pinker, *The Better Angels of Our Nature: Why Violence Has Declined* (New York: Penguin Group, 2012).

19 Bill Gates, "Dear Class of 2017 . . .," *GatesNotes*, May 15, 2017, www.gatesnotes.com/About-Bill-Gates/Dear-Class-of-2017.

of diseases that may spread more effectively than Ebola."[20] In the article, Gates offers prudential advice that would have helped contain the current global pandemic: an improved health system, trained personnel in various fields, equipment, sufficient medical supplies, and good data, which is something to which he gives particular importance. Since Gates already knew the world was ill-prepared for Covid-19, in April 2020, on a television show, he pledged to use billions of dollars from his foundation to fund laboratories working separately on a vaccine. And as late as August 2020, the Bill & Melinda Gates Foundation said it was backing the world's largest vaccine maker Serum Institute of India, to produce 100 million doses of coronavirus vaccine for poorer countries and price them at less than $3.[21]

There is something rigidly utilitarian about Gates's charity. If it does not satisfy what the philosopher Francis Bacon referred to as "the relief of man's estate" through technological and scientific progress, then Gates is not interested.[22] In fact, the Gates foundation avoids traditional avenues of philanthropy, such as the fine arts. Some argue, in fact, that when it comes to the arts, Gates is blind.[23] In a 2015 initiative, the Gates foundation brought together 30 world-renowned musicians, writers, filmmakers, painters, sculptors, and photographers, for the purpose of demonstrating how vaccines positively change the course of history.[24] Function trumps form.

Gates's philosophical and ethical modernism make it difficult see him fully devoted to the philosophical life, as outlined by Plato. One of the tenets of the philosophical life is the exalted role of *schole* or leisure. The justification for this ideal was the notion that the soul awakens through particular experiences of beauty, which lead in an upward trajectory to the ideal of Beauty. In Plato, and ancient philosophy more generally, the love of wisdom requires an ascent from tangible experiences toward the higher reflective ideals. A budding philosopher's wonder feeds on gratuitous experiences, ones that spark the movement from the shadows of the Cave to the light of the Sun.

---

20 Bill Gates, "The Next Epidemic: Lessons from Ebola," *New England Journal of Medicine* 372, no. 15 (2015): 1381–4.

21 Eric Bellman, "Gates Foundation Teams Up with Vaccine Maker to Produce $3 Covid-19 Shots," *The Wall Street Journal*, August 7, 2020, www.wsj.com/articles/gates-foundation-teams-up-with-vaccine-maker-to-produce-3-covid-19-shots-11596804573.

22 Francis Bacon, *The Advancement of Learning*, ed. Henry Morley (London: Cassell & Company, 1893), retrieved from Project Gutenberg, www.gutenberg.org/files/5500/5500-h/5500-h.htm.

23 Terry Teachout, "What Bill Gates Is Blind to," *The Wall Street Journal*, November 21, 2013, www.wsj.com/articles/SB10001424052702303531204579205770596464870.

24 "Press Release and Statements," The Bill and Melinda Gates Foundation, accessed January 6, 2021, www.gatesfoundation.org/Media-Center/Press-Releases/2015/01/The-Art-of-Saving-a-Life-Project.

The classical appreciation of the comingling of goodness and beauty for philosophy is uncommon in our modern world, especially in the pragmatically oriented United States. Bill Gates, like most Americans, cannot be faulted for something that his passions are not attuned to. But we do not think that Gates is inured completely to the philosophical ideal of aligning the eye of the soul to the highest Good, as even Gates betrays his seemingly narrow concern for utility. In 1994, well on his way to becoming the richest man on earth, Bill Gates spent $23 million on Leonardo da Vinci's "Codex Leicester," a 72-page notebook including commentary on issues from geology to the science of water, from astronomy to technology. Why did Gates purchase this work? Did he crave status or see it as an investment opportunity? Or was he interested in mining Da Vinci's notebook for new ideas? Doubtful. Gates shares in that rare sense of wonder that grabs hold of the potential philosopher in Plato's *Republic*. In an interview he gave in 2013, Gates said about Leonardo and the notebook: it is "an inspiration that one person – off on their own, with no feedback, without being told what was right or wrong – that he kept pushing himself, that he found knowledge itself to be the most beautiful thing."[25]

In the end, Gates is a modern-day truth-seeker and a thought leader in his own right. As a paradigmatic thinker, he looks for patterns and organizes his thoughts, but also sticks to the surface because he is data-driven. Intelligence is malleable and will continue to grow and change through discovery and innovation. Gates's leadership aims at a true education, as we identified it in Chapter 2. He lives to share his intelligence and others' ideas by amplifying and building on them – one idea, cause, or innovation at a time.

Case study two: Nelson Mandela

We argued in Chapter 3 that Aristotle's idea of greatness of soul expresses something that is exceptional yet alive with possibility. It speaks not only to formal and conscious character, emotional control, and deliberate decision making, but also to the connection to the body, one's place within a harmonious cosmos, and all the poignant things that sculpt and pattern the soul consciously and unconsciously. Greatness of soul, we believe, can help illuminate remarkable human types whose leadership resonates beyond their times. Our task here, as the authors, is to graft a modern shoot on to this ancient rootstock.

Our idea of a great-souled leader is that he is inflexibly principled even in the midst of uncertainty and fear in society. His role is in high-politics

---

25 Bill Gates 2.0, *60 Minutes*, CBS, May, 14, 2013.

because greatness of soul involves the highest stakes, the survival and direction of the political community. He takes the moral high ground and waits there patiently, creating the atmosphere for everyone around him to catch up. Crucial to his success are social virtues that orbit around his soul's greatness, such as ambition, patience, gentleness, charm, wit, and friendliness. He does not renounce glory and praise, but as a great-souled leader, he handles these recognitions with grace, which helps him bear responsibility with great seriousness. Thanks to his self-control, he is not imperious but helps others take on responsibility and share in his moral imagination.

In South Africa, in the late 20th century, the country needed to pull off a political miracle and unite a country headed to either the continued and violent domination of one race over another or bloody civil war. For 18 years, while housed at Robben Island off the coast of Cape Town, in an 8-foot by 7-foot concrete cell with only a straw mat to sleep on, a man was integrating all his character virtues and forming the great soul that South Africa needed. On February 11, 1990, the eyes of the world were fixed on this man as he emerged from prison.

Nelson Mandela, known to black South Africans as "Madiba," is recent history's great-souled leader. He brought peace and reconciliation to South Africa during its democratic transition and post-apartheid era. He is considered the father of South African democracy and the nation. Many even called him "*Tata*," a Xhosa word for father. Archbishop Desmond Tutu, a Nobel peace prize winner like Mandela, was once asked if he could define Mandela's most outstanding quality: "Tutu thought for a moment and then – triumphantly – uttered one word: magnanimity. 'Yes,' he repeated, more solemnly the second time, almost in a whisper. 'Magnanimity!'"[26]

In his lifetime, Mandela became globally famous for his commitment to the anti-apartheid struggle, arrest and subsequent 27-year imprisonment, eventual release at 70 years old, and becoming president of South Africa in 1994. The cornerstone of Mandela's achievement was negotiating the country's democratic transition and an end to apartheid without bloodshed. Before his imprisonment in 1962, Mandela had advocated for armed struggle and seemed headed down the 20th-century Marxist-Leninist firebrands' path. With his long imprisonment, death of many anti-apartheid leaders in the 1970s and 1980s, and increasing brutality of the South African police state, the natural course of politics seemed to lend itself to Mandela favoring a radical approach: a full transfer of power to South African blacks, expropriation of white-owned land, and widespread criminal trials of government

26 John Carlin, "Nelson Mandela: The Freedom Fighter Who Embraced His Enemies," *Guardian*, 2013, www.theguardian.com/world/2013/dec/07/nelson-mandela-freedom-fighter-john-carlin.

officials responsible for the worst abuses under apartheid. Rather than try to balance the scales and punish the enablers of such an oppressive regime, he made the opposite choice and sought peace and racial reconciliation with the enemy.

Assuming the presidency in 1994, Mandela avoided a civil war by moderating the black electorate's understandable bitterness while reassuring whites, with their fears of retribution and nationalist fervor, that there was a future for them in South Africa. Black Africans comprised seventy percent of the population. Over two centuries, they fought nine wars in a row with Dutch English settlers, culminating in the great Zulu War of 1879. South Africa's largest black (*bantu*) tribes consisted of the: Zulu, Xhosa, and Sotho. South Africa's white minority were descendants of Dutch settlers living on the continent's southern tip since 1651. They spoke Afrikaans, which was derived from Dutch and used nowhere else in the world. As a group, these Afrikaners saw themselves as heirs to a promised land that their ancestors had fought for in wars against Zulu, Ndebele, and other tribes. They belonged to the Dutch Reformed Church and tended to be farmers and controlled politics, the police, and armed forces. The Afrikaners ruled the country with an uncompromising commitment to racial *apartheid* (apartness), originally an English practice but institutionalized and enforced by the Afrikaners. The English descendants, an even smaller group, had control over most of the businesses in South Africa and were deeply resented by Afrikaners. People deemed "officially Coloured" descended from laborers imported from Indonesia and Malaya.

We argue that Mandela's great soul helped project onto South Africans the deeply felt conviction that political moderation was the best possible outcome for the common good. Mandela led South Africa to a principled compromise. He accomplished this task by embracing the Afrikaners, deciding on this plan while a prisoner. He made the choice independently and, first, in secret. It was a prudential choice that took great courage. Mandela was the leader of black Africans, but he understood the plight, fears, and histories of Afrikaners. The ANC (African Nationalist Congress) and other black leadership were not ready to commit to such a step.

Mandela stood for political moderation, which is something that does not generate enthusiasm and may also spark suspicion. He understood that remorseless revolutionary struggle would not benefit anyone, while zealousness to right past injustices could quickly get out of hand. He was once asked if he favored the prosecution of men who had carried out murders on behalf of the government. Mandela answered: "No, no, no. The whole spirit of negotiations would be against taking revenge on any particular individual. You think of a settlement as involving the entire community in support of the settlement. Otherwise, it will be an intolerable situation."[27]

One writer has argued that Mandela's greatness of soul was characterized principally by the Christian virtue of forgiveness.[28] The following question was put to him in 2007, in an interview for his obituary: "after such barbarous torment, how do you keep hatred in check? – his answer was almost dismissive: Hating clouds the mind. It gets in the way of strategy."[29] There is no doubt that a Christian ethic pervades Mandela's leadership, but the road to his great souled leadership was long and complicated. Mandela accepted his calling as a servant leader, but we argue that his deliberate character formation and disposition is squarely of an Aristotelian mold.[30]

A great-souled leader must be a good and just person who has a balanced set of desires and aggressive instincts, all of which are controlled and shaped by reason.[31] Mandela's forgiveness was deliberate or, as he said, strategic, and his temper was a product of a character that he mastered in prison. Mandela's greatness of soul was the product of his intellect and introspection, and, at the same time, he had the bearing of a gentlemen his entire life. Mandela also had natural gifts and characteristics, including his formidable size, and delicate and handsome looks, which gave splendor to his deliberate grace and polish. He possessed a keen memory and took command of social settings by his ability to read people. Moreover, his lifelong commitment to discipline helped him develop legendary self-control.[32] One of the marks of a great-souled man is an accompaniment of social virtues and graces, one of which is gentleness. The gentle person "wishes to be calm and not led by his passion, but rather as reason may command, and so to be harsh regarding the things he ought and for the requisite time"

27 Anthony Lewis, "Abroad at Home: Miracle with Reasons," *New York Times*, April 29, 1994, Gale in Context: Science.
28 See David Aikman, *Great Souls: Six Who Changed the Century* (Lanham, MD: Lexington Books, 2003), 60–124.
29 Bill Keller, "Nelson Mandela, South Africa's Liberator as Prisoner and President, Dies at 95," *New York Times*, December 5, 2013, www.nytimes.com/2013/12/06/world/africa/nelson-mandela_obit.html.
30 For an examination of Nelson Mandela as an exemplar of servant leadership, see Charles John Baker, *Servant Leadership: The Case of Nelson Mandela* (London, UK: SAGE Publications Limited, 2017).
31 Gerard J. Hughes, *Routledge Philosophy Guidebook to Aristotle on Ethics* (New York: Routledge, 2001), 90.
32 Nigel Nicholson, "Mandela's Lessons in Self-Leadership," *London Business School*, December 5, 2017, www.london.edu/think/mandelas-lessons-in-self-leadership.

(1125b35–1126a1).[33] These qualities and poignant life experiences fused a sophisticated inner complexity that Mandela would then project into a plain-spoken and modest public image. Mandela was anything but ordinary, however. He never strayed from a depth of purpose and carefully and deliberately made his choices, and he did this without ever appearing strained.

A full-length case of Mandela's life and leadership is not possible here.[34] We aim, instead, to stitch together the crucial biographical episodes that we think trace the arc of Mandela's formation into a great-souled leader, which culminated in prison. In prison, Mandela's powerful character gradually developed into a great-souled man, master politician, and mediator of the minority White Dutch-speaking Afrikans, the majority African blacks of many tribal identities, and minority Coloureds and Indians. In this section, we pay close attention to the following elements that comprise his life: Mandela's Xhosa tradition, education in missionary schools, life in Johannesburg, gradual politicization, turn to militancy, and personal transformation through imprisonment.

Rolihlahla (meaning shaker of trees) Dahlibunga Mandela was born in 1918, in Mvezo, a small village in the Transkei, 600 miles south of Johannesburg. A bucolic countryside, the Transkei was a nominally independent state that was set aside for the Xhosa and home of the Thembu people, a subgroup of the Xhosa. Through his father, Gadla Hendry Mphakanyswa, Nelson Mandela was a minor royal. Hendry Mandela, illiterate, pagan, and polygamous, was the hereditary chief of Mvezo and principal counselor to the acting king of the Thembu. Tribal leadership was traditional but not strictly hierarchical as it emphasized collectivity and consensus, lending a democratic versatility to Xhosa traditions. His mother, one of four of Hendry's wives, was a devout Methodist. Mandela was groomed to be in the royal council to the king at an early age, like his father. As a rural aristocrat, Mandela participated in a Xhosa man's traditional rearing, including sport, horse riding, dancing to tribal songs, oral tradition, and circumcision, a crucial rite of passage for males.

Mandela learned about leadership from the Xhosa's oral tradition, replete with stories of ancestral heroes. Xhosa storytellers were creative performers who articulated a comprehensive moral universe and praised chiefs and

---

33 As was the case in Chapter Three, the translation we have used is: Aristotle, *Aristotle's Nicomachean Ethics*, trans., with an interpretive essay, notes, and glossary, Robert C. Bartlett and Susan D. Collins (Chicago: University of Chicago Press, 2011).

34 On the life of Nelson Mandela one can consult his famous autobiography, Nelson Mandela, *Long Walk to Freedom* (New York: Roaring Brook Press, 2009). For the authorized biography of Mandela, see Anthony Sampson, *Mandela: The Authorized Biography* (New York: Knopf, 1999).

warriors. These storytellers told the entire world of the Xhosa people, how they first came to be, the origins of their customs, and how they manage all of life's transitions from birth to death.[35] The Xhosa praise poets wore elaborate outfits and were highly skilled and knowledgeable of history, current events, and tribal lineages. While the praise poets' intention was laudatory, inspiring the audience to be loyal to a chief, they also had a license to criticize chiefs if they failed to govern according to the Xhosa moral code.[36] The Xhosa oral tradition is reminiscent of ancient Greek *aoidoi* or bards, who created poems on traditional subjects each time they performed.

After his father's death, at age 9, Mandela became the ward of the Thembu Regent, Jongintaba, who was also a devout Methodist. He moved to a new large home called the Great Place, where Mandela spent a good deal of time observing the Regent, who applied the African ideal human brotherhood, or *ubuntu*, in his tribal deliberations.[37] Under the support of his guardian, Mandela also attended church, wore western clothes, and received a British education, where he was introduced to English, the written Xhosa language, history, and geography. Mandela's cloistered youth, away from whites in a nominally free Xhosa enclave, was an exciting combination of Xhosa culture, aristocratic grooming, English education, and a consensus approach to leadership. "As a leader," Mandela wrote, "I have always followed the principle I first saw demonstrated by the regent at the Great Place."[38]

From the ages of 16 to 22, Mandela underwent a profound life transition as he was sent away and attended rigorous missionary schools: Clarkebury and Healdtown. There he encountered not only English men he respected but also educated African teachers and young African students, both male and female. Here he found himself in a community that respected merit and intelligence more than hereditary status.[39] In 1939, Mandela was sent off to an exclusive university, Fort Hare. Here, Mandela was introduced to politics and law and took up cross-country running and boxing. Not a natural sportsman, Mandela was seriously committed to training and made a daily regime of exercise part of his life, which became crucial to him in prison. Mandela only spent 1 year at Hare because he refused to serve on the

35 Nongenile M. Zenani, *The World and the Word: Tales and Observations from the Xhosa Oral Tradition* (Madison: University of Wisconsin Press, 1992).
36 Mhlobo Jadezweni, "Two Xhosa Praise Poets in Performance: The Dawn of a New Era," *University of Leipzig Papers on Africa, Languages and Literatures Series*, No. 09 (1999).
37 See Daryll Forde, *African Worlds: Studies in the Cosmological Ideas and Social Values of African Peoples* (Suffolk, UK: James Currey, 1999); Segun Gbadegesin, *African Philosophy: Traditional Yoruba Philosophy and Contemporary African Realities* (New York: Peter Lang, 1991).
38 Michael Cassidy, *A Witness Forever* (London: Hodder and Stoughton, 1995), 16.
39 Anthony Sampson, *Mandela* (New York: Vintage Books, 2000), 19.

student representative council, as a large share of the students boycotted the election. Mandela, at 23, returned to the Great Place. Upon his return, and after a complicated set of circumstances, including plans for an arranged marriage, he and the Regent's son, Justice, ran away to Johannesburg.

Arriving in 1941, with nothing but a suit and his gentlemen's demeanor, life in Johannesburg opened a new chapter in Mandela's life. Initially aloof from politics, he witnessed firsthand the discontent and anger of Blacks who lived in destitute segregated townships, had no political power, and faced daily indignities of the apartheid system. In Soweto, the black township of Johannesburg, blacks were considered temporary visitors and only food could be bought there. Everything else was available for purchase in Johannesburg, in a white-owned store, a ten mile bus ride away. No black could own land in Soweto or acquire a permanent title to a house. The most unpopular of the apartheid laws were the Pass Laws. At age 16, every black African had to carry a pass book with his or her person and produce it on demand to a policeman. One can imagine how Mandela's proud demeanor and aristocratic country identity were put to the test as he became an anonymous and voiceless *kaffir*, the term of insult for Black Africans, in a large city.

Mandela's professional ambition was to be a lawyer. He became friends with Walter Sisulu, who became his lifelong friend, and he helped him get a job as a clerk with Lazer Sidelsky, a Jewish South African lawyer and activist. In this early urban period, he would also marry his first wife, Evelyn Mase, and father three children with her. They eventually divorced in 1956, a process that Mase initiated. By 1942, Mandela had finished his bachelor's degree through correspondence and was even allowed to return to Fort Hare for his graduation ceremony, and in 1943 he enrolled in law school and gradually became involved in politics. He wrote: "There was no particular day on which I said, From henceforth I will devote myself to the liberation of my people; instead, I simply found myself doing so, and could not do otherwise."[40] In 1944, Mandela intensified his politics by spearheading a youth league for the ANC.

By the 1950s, Mandela became immersed in politics. He undertook a serious study of political theory, reading Western philosophers, South African liberals, black nationalists, Gandhi, and Nehru. He also read Marx, as did most African nationalists at that time, and about Marx's philosophy, he said it "seemed to offer both a searchlight illuminating the dark night of racial oppression and a tool that could be used to end it."[41]

---

40 Cassidy, *Witness Forever*, 84.
41 Mandela, *Long Walk to Freedom,* 120.

Meanwhile, ANC membership had grown to 100,000 and Mandela was orga-nizing and participating in protests and boycotts. He said he no longer felt "overwhelmed by the power and seeming invincibility of the white man and his institutions. . . . But now the white man felt the power of my punches and I could walk upright like a man."[42] He was "banned" multiple times from participating with the ANC by the Nationalist government, which served to cut off key leaders from political participation. One story worth recounting here is a speech Mandela gave in 1952 for the Youth League, in which he pre-dicted that he would become the first black president of South Africa. At the time, many audience members, especially senior leaders, dubbed the speech as mere arrogance, yet many would live to see the prediction come true.[43] The young Mandela had ambition and *thumotic* energy in his youth, a fire in his belly that he would learn to harness and temper with time.

In 1953, Mandela opened the first African-owned law firm with his part-ner Oliver Tambo. Between his activities at the ANC and the law firm's massive workload, Mandela used his legendary discipline to meet demands. Rising every day at 4:00 am, he exercised vigorously and then got on with his workload for the remainder of the day. At night, he also sparred as an amateur boxer. With a successful law firm, Mandela began to don stylish suits. Mandela was always a meticulous dresser and carefully cultivated an aesthetic well into his presidency. He wore shirts that symbolized liberation and were woven with Javanese silk batik or African fabrics.[44]

The ANC's increasing militancy and embrace of communism led to the government's banning of the group first and jailing 155 of its leaders and activists, including Mandela, in 1956. The government charged the leaders with high treason, and the 5-year proceedings became famously known as the Treason Trial. In 1960, Mandela and other prisoners' acquittal led to the South African Nationalist government's abandoning of a legal strategy to oppose the ANC and turned to its police force instead. 1960–1962 marked the most militant point of Mandela's life. He was appointed Commander in Chief of the ANC's secreted armed wing, known as *Umkhonto we Sizwe* (Spear of the Nation). Mandela operated in the underground and studied Che Guevara's and Mao Tsetung's tactics while also studying von Clause-witz's classic, "On War."

The armed wing's first plan was to plant homemade bombs in South Afri-can installations and symbolic targets. Over the years, the groups detonated

---

42 Cassidy, *Witness Forever*, 83.
43 Joe Matthews, "The Long Walk of Nelson Mandela," interview by John Carlin, *Frontline*, www.pbs.org/wgbh/pages/frontline/shows/mandela/revolution/matthews.html.
44 Emilie Gambade, "Chronicles of Chic: Mandela, Man of Style," *Daily Maverick*, 2020, www.dailymaverick.co.za/article/2013-07-18-chronicles-of-chic-mandela-man-of-style.

several bombs. At 44, Mandela became South Africa's most wanted man, and the press dubbed him the Black Pimpernel. Mandela became a disguise artist: "my most frequent disguise was as a chauffeur, a chef, or a 'garden boy.' I would wear the blue overalls of the fieldworker and often wore round, rimless glasses known as Mazzawati teaglass."[45] He even disguised himself as a garage worker and wheeled a spare tire down the main street of Johannesburg under the nose of the cops.[46]

Mandela envisaged a larger role for the ANC's armed wing, and he escaped the country, traveled to Africa and Europe, and, lastly, underwent military training in Ethiopia for 8 weeks. He genuinely expected to build a guerilla army but was recalled by the ANC in 1962, and not soon after his return Mandela was arrested. The court sentenced Mandela to 5 years in prison for leaving the country illegally and inciting strikes. He used the proceedings to deliver his most electrifying political speech:

> I hate race discrimination most intensely and in all its manifestations. I have fought it all during my life; I fight it now, and will do so until the end of my days. Even although I now happen to be tried by one whose opinion I hold in high esteem, I detest most violently the set-up that surrounds me here. It makes me feel that I am a black man in a white man's court.[47]

Within a few months, however, Mandela and other political prisoners were linked to their planning for guerrilla warfare. They were given life imprisonment and transferred from Pretoria to Robben Island, 9 kilometers off the coast of Cape Town. Upon arriving on June 15, 1964, the white warders shouted at them in Afrikaans, "This is the island! Here you will die."[48] Mandela was 46.

Robben Island housed South Africa's most dangerous criminals. They were made to labor in a quarry, crushing limestone and filling barrels daily under the sun's exposure. There was no rest during work hours. Communication between prisoners was banned, and prisoners could only send or receive letters, which were scrutinized and censored, every 6 months. The

45 Nelson Mandela, "The Revolutionary: 'The Black Pimpernel'," chap. 40 in *Long Walk to Freedom* (Boston, MA: Little, Brown and Company, 1994), *Frontline*, www.pbs.org/wgbh/pages/frontline/shows/mandela/revolution/living.html.
46 "South Africa: The Black Pimpernel," *Time*, August 17, 1962, accessed January 13, 2021, http://content.time.com/time/subscriber/article/0,33009,870031,00.html.
47 United Nations, "'Black Man in a White Court': Nelson Mandela's First Court Statement-1962," www.un.org/en/events/mandeladay/court_statement_1962.shtml.
48 Tom Lodge, *A Critical Life* (Oxford: Oxford University Press, 2007), 107.

warders controlled all aspects of the prisoners' lives, even down to the speed at which they walked of used punishments to induce behavior. Mandela eschewed outbursts of anger and demonstrated to his fellow prisoners' deliberate ways of defiance that preserved their dignity. Mandela challenged the warders, who were the most unrepentant racists, on every single indignity. Slowly, he began to exert his will over the warders by insisting that they respect his dignity, a lesson that Mandela would use when confronted by his political enemies upon release. Mandela was able to deliberately lead his fellow prisoners by practicing self-control and persisting with his regimented way of life. In his tiny prison cell, twice a week, he would begin with running on the spot for 45 minutes, followed by 100 fingertip push-ups, 200 sit-ups, 50 deep knee-bends, and callisthenic exercises learned from his gym training. Mandela continued to exercise despite the grueling manual labor in the quarry. For Mandela, vigorous exercise was not only for good physical condition but also to keep strict discipline in his life.[49]

Like a classical Stoic, Mandela's emotional control and persistence led him to go from survivor to the leader at Robben Island. For years, he petitioned and finally won the right for an end to forced labor and many freedoms for prisoners such as study, correspondence, and limited visitation. As more youthful and rebellious prisoners began to arrive at Robben Island, Mandela turned his Stoic attitude toward them, seeking to influence them to his ways. Mandela was not merely fighting for better accommodations; he was consciously preparing for the day when he would have to sit down and negotiate the transition to democracy and try to persuade the Nationalist government to give up power rather than fight to a brutal end. Mandela reached this understanding in prison and used the interactions with his jailers and the prison heads as a testing ground, drawing a blueprint of the Afrikaner personality.[50] And to the dismay of his fellow political prisoners, he learned Afrikaner history and language. Without a doubt Mandela suffered in prison, but we contend that it became the crucible that deepened him and prepared him for the significant future challenge in political leadership that lay ahead.

Mandela took time to learn about himself in prison and intertwined such soul searching with learning about political greatness. He and other political prisoners were fond of Shakespeare, reciting long tracts of their favorite

---

49 See Nelson Mandela, *Long Walk to Freedom: The Autobiography of Mandela* (New York: Little Brown and Company, 1994).
50 David Schalkwyk, "Mandela, the Emotions, and the Lessons of Prison," in *The Cambridge Companion to Nelson Mandela*, ed. Rita Barnard (Cambridge: Cambridge University Press, 2014), 50–69.

plays. All the inmates autographed their favorite passages; Mandela chose one from Julius Caesar:

> *Cowards die many times before their deaths;*
> *The valiant never taste of death but once.*
> *Of all the wonders that I yet have heard,*
> *It seems to me most strange that men should fear,*
> *Seeing that death, a necessary end,*
> *Will come when it will come.*[51]

Essential to Mandela and the other prisoners was the opportunity to study, and the quarry became known as the "university at Robben Island."[52] Mandela became famous for his political economy lectures, in which he used a Socratic method that left some of its participants "bloodied and humiliated."[53] Mandela read voraciously and widely. Major authors included Steinbeck, Dostoevsky, and Tolstoy. He also read Afrikaans poetry, and Wordsworth, Tennyson, and Shelley among the English poets. And, as his fellow prisoner Eric Moloboi described: "While the comrades were reading *Das Kapital*, Madiba was reading Churchill's war memoirs, or biographies of Keeny or Vorster."[54] According to Mandela's biographer, he

> also read biographies of Lincoln, Washington, Disraeli and several Boer War leaders, including Smuts and Koos de la Rey; but the one who really fascinated him was Christiaan de Wet, who led the 1914 rebellion. While the Afrikaner government was accusing Mandela of being a communist, he was studying not Marx but their own heroes.[55]

Mandela, it seems, was reading, studying, and meditating on the topic of the "great man," and he also turned to classical literature. In a 1985 letter, he noted, "We are still fascinated by Greek literature of ancient times."[56] At Robben Island, the prisoners performed Greek tragedies and Mandela played the tyrant Creon in Jean Anouilh's version of Antigone.[57] Mandela's long arc from a childhood of Xhosa heroic poetry to the Greeks, Christian missionary schools to African Nationalism, Marxism to an African

---

51 Cited in Sampson, *Mandela*, 231.
52 Sampson, *Mandela*, 233.
53 Sampson, *Mandela*, 234.
54 Sampson, *Mandela*, 282.
55 Sampson, *Mandela*, 282.
56 Schalkwyk, "Mandela, the Emotions, and the Lessons of Prison," 58.
57 Schalkwyk, "Mandela, the Emotions, and the Lessons of Prison," 58.

(communitarian) understanding of liberalism, allowed him to free himself from any strict tribal identity or modern ideology. Through patience and reason, Mandela practiced a virtue of unshakeable openness, leading those who opposed him (white and black) eventually to side with his position.

It is of little wonder why the theme of Mandela's favorite poem *Invictus* (unconquered), written by the Victorian poet William Henley, is about conquering circumstances through strength of character. Mandela was a remarkable man. He practiced the highest degree of human responsibility, self-discipline, and self-awareness. By becoming a great souled leader, he held a mirror up to all others to exercise, if not imitate, his high-minded citizenship. Mandela was not a typical man of his age, as neither was Winston Churchill, Abraham Lincoln, or Pericles. Like all these other great souled leaders, Mandela was a political man, leading in a democratic regime during a period of turbulence. He, like these others, inhabited his political world but transcended it, too. In the end, Mandela points to the possibility of the great souled leader's self-sufficiency, on one hand, but someone who is also motivated to act to improve others' political and moral lots, on the other.

Case study three: Al Dunlap

As we argued in Chapter 4, we are heirs of Machiavelli's untrodden path: a new and enterprising vision of human behavior, decision-making, and the ethical dilemma of dirty hands – the idea that leaders transgress moral principles because the position demands it. And the modern firm is an exciting testing ground for these issues under a CEO's leadership. The CEO balances opposing forces, the internal stakeholders' well-being, such as employees and managers, and the interests of shareholders, who own a stake in the public company as stock. Given these unique circumstances guiding a firm and its investors, the CEO is putatively the company's steward; she seeks to lead a company and its employees, on one hand, while exercising responsibility to the investors, on the other. Nevertheless, the CEO is also an ambitious person who stands to gain from a firm's success by monetary compensation, reputation, and control over its operations. Given their essential responsibilities and own stakes in a company, CEOs occupy a role about which scholars of leadership are especially curious.[58] What is the work of the CEO, and what are her ethical responsibilities? Here we focus on the CEO responsibility, especially the case where the CEO does not demonstrate self-sacrificing instincts. In such cases, it would be easy to

---

58 Peter F. Drucker, "What Makes an Effective Executive," *Harvard Business Review Magazine*, 2004, https://hbr.org/2004/06/what-makes-an-effective-executive.

label them poor leaders, but does that truly describe the nuanced portraits of leaders who behave badly? A Machiavellian understanding of corporate leaders could broaden our knowledge without requiring us to exculpate bad leadership.

One notorious CEO of the 1990s, Al "Chainsaw" Dunlap, personifies some of Machiavelli's teachings, such as cruelty well used, fear over love, and the beast and man. Al Dunlap rose to fame because of his seemingly remarkable turn-arounds of companies in dire financial straits by aggressive downsizing. His strategy sacrificed everything, mainly people, for the sake of financials that excited investors. Dunlap rose to prominence when, in 1994, he increased the share of Scott Paper by 225%, which he accomplished by cutting 11,000 employees, or 35% of its workforce. He then arranged for the sale of Scott to its number one competitor Kimberly-Clark. His combined earnings at Scott netted him $100 million. Dunlap's career ended ignominiously after an accounting scandal at Sunbeam Corporation. John A. Byrne documents Dunlap's career and eventual fall at Sunbeam in his book *Chainsaw*.[59]

Dunlap's notoriety for firing people gave rise to his nickname, "Chainsaw Al," although his preferred moniker was "Rambo in pinstripes." In public, Dunlap espoused that his philosophy was aligned with market capitalism's ultimate goal, which is that the corporation is ultimately responsible to the shareholders who assume all the risk. In his view, as he once said in an interview about corporate responsibility, downsizing companies with severe financial difficulties, such as Scott, saves jobs: the remaining 65% of employees.[60] But Dunlap's view implies that the surviving employees share his belief and, consequently, become grateful for being spared. As Dunlap recounted in his autobiography, *Mean Business: How I Save Bad Companies and Make Good Companies*, he did not seem concerned with saving jobs. Rather, resembling in some sense Machiavelli's notion of cruelty well used, Dunlap relished the opportunity to fire people and make examples of them.

What explains a specimen like Al Dunlap, someone whose words and treatment of others, in the estimation of those who observe common decency, were unsympathetic and callous? Dunlap came from obscure origins. Born in Hoboken, New Jersey, in 1937, he was the first student in his town ever to attend West Point and graduated in 1960, 537th of 550 in his

---

59 John A. Byrne, *Chainsaw: The Notorious Career of Al Dunlap in the Era of Profit-at-Any-Price* (New York: Harper Business, 1999).

60 See Paul Tough and Al Dunlap on CNN, May 9, 1996, discussing the Harper's Magazine Forum on corporate responsibility, www.paultough.com/2013/02/paul-tough-on-corporate-responsibility-part-one.

cadet class.[61] After serving 3 years of mandated military service, he landed his first job with Kimberly-Clark, and 4 years later, he became the manager of Sterling Pulp and Paper Co. Here he began his practice of laying off workers to reduce costs, which he turned into his singular purpose and applied to each of his jobs for the next three decades. According to Barbara Kellerman, for each of these companies, he proved a "faithful and effective hatchet man, cutting and slashing his way to success."[62]

Viewed as a "celebrity downsizer," Dunlap was an atavism of the 1980s Michael Douglas's character Gordon Gekko, in *Wall Street* (1987), who portrays a ruthless financial leader famous for saying "greed is good." In *Mean Business*, he offers his management advice, which is neither beguiling nor fascinating. His many maxims are evidence of his aggressive executive style, which include: "fire all consultants; I put a high premium on loyalty; if you see an annual report with the term 'stakeholders,' put it down and run."

Dunlap's advice does not give itself over to sophistication. Still, he managed to attract critical decision-makers to him during his career because Wall Street rewarded his draconian downsizings. After all, he focused solely on value creation (shareholder value). Although he gained a reputation for his callousness and became intensely disliked, Wall Street viewed him as "a brutal but efficient turnaround artist."[63] Thus, it is these competing moral interpretations of Al Dunlap that require a subtler Machiavellian analysis. Returning to the lessons for a prince, we ask did Dunlap practice the vices that help him keep his state (maximum control over the company) and avoid the infamy of vices that would lead him to lose his state? Or roughly stated, was Dunlap a modern-day prince in his capacity as CEO?

By all accounts, Dunlap was a restive CEO who would quickly become bored if a business did not present a challenge, which is why he relished the opportunity to take over companies in crisis. Despite his success, Dunlap retained this restless ambition his whole life. Dunlap's self-description evinces the prince's primordial understanding of necessity. He once said, "Strip me naked, put me out on the street, and I'm going to survive."[64]

Nevertheless, Dunlap deliberately joined troubled companies because they suited his quick and bold style. Troubled companies are not just those with a looming financial crisis, but also ones with problems in leadership

61 Barbara Kellerman, *Bad Leadership: What It Is, How It Happens, Why It Matters* (Cambridge: Harvard Business Press, 2004), 132.

62 Kellerman, *Bad Leadership*, 133.

63 Joseph Nocera, "Confessions of a Corporate Killer," *Fortune*, September 30, 1996, https://archive.fortune.com/magazines/fortune/fortune_archive/1996/09/30/217401/index.htm.

64 Byrne, *Chainsaw*, 28.

and management, trust, and morale. Dunlap entered such climates with an intuitive understanding of Machiavellian leadership: he would take charge of these companies and rely on his own arms, figuratively. Never did he cede control by adopting the existing corporate culture. Dunlap executed this strategy by purging the ranks, which he also used as an opportunity to leave an impression on his employees. Much like a performer who is aware of the stage, as the new CEO, Dunlap had to impose the theatrical distance between himself, the lead, and the bit actors, the other Sunbeam employees.

Byrne recounts Dunlap's first meeting with the corporate staff at Sunbeam in detail:

> At precisely 9 A.M. . . . Albert J. Dunlap marched into the room without introduction, without issuing a single greeting to any of the anxious men around the table. . . . He wore his pinstripes like a military uniform, meticulously pressed, without a single wrinkle or a stray thread. . . . The silver-haired Dunlap also wore a severe look on his face . . . his hard blue eyes, hidden by dark glasses, canvassed the room, fixing on each one of them.[65]

Donning the mantle of a corporate prophet, Dunlap seizes the opportunity to define the moral climate for the purge that he will eventually set in motion: "This is the best day of your life if you are good at what you do and are willing to accept change, and it's the worst day of your life if you're not."[66] During that first day, Dunlap dressed down his executive staff, blaming them for Sunbeam's losses, and by the end of the first day, he fired James Clegg, the chief operating officer.

Dunlap's behavior at Sunbeam was not new. At Scott Paper, he claimed to have fired 9 of 11 people on the executive committee in the first week. According to one executive at Scott, "everyone talked about him. He put the fear of God into a lot of people. When he was in the building his presence was palpable."[67] He did not only induce fear, but also liked to speak in maxims. In a 1996 interview, during his tenure at Sunbeam, he said, "It's better to be honestly arrogant than falsely humble."[68]

Between spectacular firings, massive downsizing, and choosing fear over love, on the surface, Dunlap appears like a modern-day prince. He introduces a new order into a troubled company. Given the uncertainty, all

---

65 Byrne, *Chainsaw*, 2.
66 Byrne, *Chainsaw*, 3.
67 Byrne, *Chainsaw*, 26.
68 Herbert McCann, "Chainsaw: Al Dunlap Again Lives up to Reputation," *AP News*, November 12, 1996.

employees have a lot to lose by the arrival of a new order. Machiavelli says, "for the introducer has all those who benefit from the old order as enemies, and he has lukewarm defenders in all those who might benefit from the new orders." Like a new prince, Al Dunlap conquered, figuratively speaking, bringing in a new order into a company and using force to impose his beliefs among its employees.

As we argued in Chapter 4, the new prince who has considered "everything well" understands not only necessity but also how to use both natures, the beast and man. Recalling the lesson of the beast and man here, Machiavelli says there are two images to choose from, the fox and the lion. The lion's ferocity is always necessary, but the fox proves to be the more capable of the two since it is the mode that weds penetrating judgment to deception. The prince must appear virtuous in all regards, even if he is inauthentic at his core.

By all accounts, Al Dunlap fully integrated the lion into his leadership. However, it seems that Dunlap did not learn that such ferocity was only a mode for circumstances and instead fixated on it as a principle for life. Dunlap had one lens he saw through, predator and prey. In his book, *The Psychopath Test*, Jon Ronson, a journalist, tracked down Al Dunlap to conduct a layman's analysis of whether the former CEO displayed psychopathic traits. When Ronson arrived at Dunlap's Florida mansion, he was amazed by the many sculptures of predatory animals:

> They were everywhere: stone lions and panthers with teeth bared, eagles soaring downward, hawks with fish in their talons, and on and on, across the grounds, around the lake, in the swimming pool/health club complex, in the many rooms. There were crystal lions and onyx lions and iron lions and iron panthers and paintings of lions and sculptures of human skulls.[69]

Al Dunlap's Machiavellian animalism was not the sophisticated kind of the fox and the lion: ferocity and cleverness, force and forethought. Dunlap did not adapt to circumstances. He was too proud of past accomplishments to consider that his character and fortune are both credits to success. Eventually, Dunlap fell victim to his inflexibility and short-term strategy. In 1998, Sunbeam's board ousted him because he inflated sales numbers through questionable tactics. In 2001, the company filed for bankruptcy, and the Securities and Exchange Commission charged Dunlap with fraud. He paid a fine of $500,000 and was barred from serving as an officer or director of a public company. Dunlap died in 2019, at 81 years old.

69 Ronson, *The Psychopath Test*, 148.

Bibliography

Aikman, David. *Great Souls: Six Who Changed the Century*. Lanham, MD: Lexington Books, 2003.

Andelman, Bob, and Albert J. Dunlap. *Mean Business: How I Save Bad Companies and Make Good Companies Great*. New York: Fireside, 1997.

Aristotle. *Nicomachean Ethics*. Chicago, IL: University of Chicago Press, 2012.

Bacon, Francis. *The Advancement of Learning*. Edited by Henry Morley. London: Cassell & Company, 1893. Project Gutenberg. www.gutenberg.org/files/5500/5500-h/5500-h.htm.

Bellman, Eric. "Gates Foundation Teams Up with Vaccine Maker to Produce $3 Covid-19 Shots." *The Wall Street Journal*, August 7, 2020. www.wsj.com/articles/gatesfoundation-teams-up-with-vaccine-maker-to-produce-3-covid-19-shots-11596804573.

The Bill and Melinda Gates Foundation. "Press Release and Statements." Accessed January 6, 2021. www.gatesfoundation.org/Media-Center/Press-Releases/2015/01/The-Artof-Saving-a-Life-Project.

The Bill and Melinda Gates Foundation. "What We Do-Polio-Strategy Overview." Accessed January 6, 2021. www.gatesfoundation.org/what-we-do/global-development/polio.

Bort, Julie. "Loved and Hated: The Life and Awesomeness of Bill Gates." *Business Insider*, May 28, 2012. www.businessinsider.com/awesome-life-bill-gates-2012-5#a-mean-unfair-software-baron-9.

Byrne, John A. *Chainsaw: The Notorious Career of Al Dunlap in the Era of Profit-at-Any-Price*. New York: Harper Business, 1999.

Carlin, John. "Nelson Mandela: The Freedom Fighter Who Embraced His Enemies." *Guardian*, 2013. www.theguardian.com/world/2013/dec/07/nelson-mandela-freedom-fighter.

Cassidy, Michael. *A Witness Forever*. City of Pub: Hodder and Stoughton, 1995.

Cohen, Paul. "France's Philosopher-Presidents." *Dissent*, March 29, 2019. www.dissentmagazine.org/online_articles/frances-philosopher-presidents.

Drucker, Peter. F. "What Makes an Effective Executive." *Harvard Business Review Magazine*, 2004. https://hbr.org/2004/06/what-makes-an-effective-executive.

Francis, *Laudato Si'*. Washington, DC: United States Conference of Catholic Bishops, 2015.

Gambade, Emilie. "Chronicles of Chic: Mandela, Man of Style." *Daily Maverick*, 2020 www.dailymaverick.co.za/article/2013-07-18-chronicles-of-chic-mandelaman-of-style.

Gates, Bill. "A Bet on Humanity Worth Every Dollar." *GatesNotes*, September 20, 2019. www.gatesnotes.com/About-Bill-Gates/A-bet-on-humanity.

———. "Dear Class of 2017 . . ." *GatesNotes*, May 15, 2017. www.gatesnotes.com/About-Bill-Gates/Dear-Class-of-2017.

———. "Desert Island Discs: Bill Gates." Interview by Kirsty Young. *BBC Radio 4*, February 5, 2016. www.bbc.co.uk/programmes/b06z1zdt.

———. "Here's My Plan to Improve Our World: And How You Can Help." *Wired*, November 12, 2012. www.wired.com/2013/11/bill-gates-wired-essay.

———. "The Next Epidemic: Lessons from Ebola." *New England Journal of Medicine* 372, no. 15 (2015): 1381–84.

Gates, Bill, and Melinda Gates. "Our 2018 Annual Letter: 10 Tough Questions We Get Asked." *GatesNotes*, February 13, 2018. www.gatesnotes.com/2018-Annual-Letter.

George, Claude S. *The History of Management Thought*. Englewood Cliffs, NJ: Prentice-Hall, 1968.

GuthStaff, Robert A. "In Secret Hideaway, Bill Gates Ponders Microsoft's Future." *The Wall Street Journal*, March 28, 2005.

Hannah Bae, "Bill Gates' 40th Anniversary Email: Goal Was 'a Computer on Every Desk'." *CNNMoney*, April 6, 2015. https://money.cnn.com/2015/04/05/technology/bill-gates-email-microsoft-40-anniversary/index.html.

Hughes, Gerard J. *Routledge Philosophy Guidebook to Aristotle on Ethics*. London; New York: Routledge, 2001.

Isaacson, Walter. *The Innovators: How a Group of Inventors, Hackers, Geniuses and Geeks Created the Digital Revolution*. New York: Simon and Schuster, 2014.

Jadezweni, Mhlobo. "Two Xhosa Praise Poets in Performance, the Dawn of a New Era." *University of Leipzig Papers on Africa, Languages and Literatures Series*, no. 09, 1999.

Keller, Bill. "Nelson Mandela, South Africa's Liberator as Prisoner and President, Dies at 95." *New York Times*, December 5, 2013.

Kellerman, Barbara. *Bad Leadership: What It Is, How It Happens, Why It Matters*. Boston, MA: Harvard Business Press, 2004.

Lewis, Anthony. "Abroad at Home: Miracle with Reasons." *New York Times*, April 29, 1994. Gale In Context: Science.

Lodge, Tom. *A Critical Life*. Oxford: Oxford University Press, 2007.

Mandela, Nelson. *Long Walk to Freedom: the autobiography of Nelson Mandela*. Boston, MA: Back Bay Books, 1995.

Matthews, Joe. "The Long Walk of Nelson Mandela." Interview by John Carlin. *Frontline*. www.pbs.org/wgbh/pages/frontline/shows/mandela/revolution/matthews.

McCann, Herbert. "Chainsaw: Al Dunlap again Lives Up to Reputation." *AP News*, November 12, 1996.

Musolf, Nell. *Built for Success: The Story of Microsoft*. Mankato, MN: The Creative Company, 2008.

Nicholson, Nigel. "Mandela's Lessons in Self-Leadership." *London Business School*, December 5, 2017. www.london.edu/think/mandelas-lessons-in-self-leadership.

Nisen, Max. "9 Famous Execs Who Majored in Philosophy." *Business Insider*, January 19, 2014.

Nocera, Joseph. "Confessions of a Corporate Killer." *Fortune*, September 30, 1996. https://archive.fortune.com/magazines/fortune/fortune_archive/1996/09/30/21741/indehtm.

Pinker, Steven. *The Better Angels of Our Nature: Why Violence Has Declined*. New York: Viking Penguin, 2012.

The Project Gutenberg eBook. *The Advancement of Learning*, by Francis Bacon, Edited by Henry Morley. www.gutenberg.org/files/5500/5500-h/5500-h.htm.

Ronson, Jon. *The Psychopath Test: A Journey Through the Madness Industry*. New York: Riverhead Books, 2012.

Schalkwyk, David. "Mandela, the Emotions, and the Lessons of Prison." In *The Cambridge Companion to Nelson Mandela*, edited by Rita Barnard, 50–69. Cambridge: Cambridge University Press, 2014.

Smith, Sam Benson. "The Four Rules of Reading According to Bill Gates." *Asia Reader's Digest*. Accessed January 6, 2021.

"South Africa: The Black Pimpernel." *Time*, August 17, 1962. http://content.time.com/time/subscriber/article/03300987003100.html.

Teachout, Terry. "What Bill Gates Is Blind to." *The Wall Street Journal*, November 21, 2013. www.wsj.com/articles/SB1000142405270230353120457920577059646 4870.

Tough, Paul. "Paul Tough on Corporate Responsibility (Part One)." Accessed January 13, 2021. www.paultough.com/2013/02/paul-tough-on-corporate-responsibility-part-one.

United Nations. "'Black Man in a White Court': Nelson Mandela's First Court Statement-1962." www.un.org/en/events/mandeladay/court_statement_1962.shtml.

Zenani, Nongenile M. *The World and the Word: Tales and Observations from the Xhosa Oral Tradition*. Madison: University of Wisconsin Press, 1992.

Index